RETHINKING INFRASTRUCTURE FINANCING FOR SOUTHEAST ASIA IN THE POST-PANDEMIC ERA

Vivek Rao, Stefano Gatti, Francesca Casalini, and Mattia Pianorsi

FEBRUARY 2023

ASIAN DEVELOPMENT BANK

ADB

CONTENTS

TABLES, FIGURES, AND BOXES

Tables

Figures

Boxes

ACKNOWLEDGMENTS

The study was supported under the Asian Development Bank (ADB) Knowledge and Support Technical Assistance (TA)-9791 Strengthening Fiscal Governance and Sustainability in Public–Private Partnerships. The authors are grateful to Jose Antonio Tan III, director, Southeast Asia Department, ADB, for guidance and support in making this study possible, and to ADB for financial support.

The publication heavily draws from the earlier publications. While the long list of references is provided, the following reports written by the co-authors* contribute significantly to the background research for the paper: (i) *Government policies to enhance access to credit for infrastructure-based PPPs: an approach to classification and appraisal* (Public Money & Management, Taylor & Francis, 2017); (ii) *Project Finance in Theory and Practice: Designing, Structuring, and Financing Private and Public Projects,* Third Edition (Elsevier Academic Press, 2018); (iii) *Project Finance Collateralized Debt Obligations: An Empirical Analysis of Spread Determinants* (European Financial Management, Wiley, 2012); (iv) *Public–Private Collaborations for Long Term Investments: Converging Towards Public Value Creation* (Edward Elgar Publishing, 2022); and (v) *Public–Private Partnerships: Principles for Sustainable Contracts* (Palgrave Macmillan Cham, 2021).

* Vivek Rao, principal financial sector specialist, Southeast Asia Department; Stefano Gatti, Antin IP Professor of Infrastructure Finance, Bocconi University; Francesca Casalini, researcher and junior lecturer, Bocconi University; Mattia Pianorsi, research assistant, Bocconi University.

ABBREVIATIONS

ADB	Asian Development Bank
CLO	collateralized loan obligations
COVID-19	coronavirus disease
DFI	development finance institution
GDP	gross domestic product
GFC	global financial crisis
G20	Group of Twenty
MDB	multilateral development bank
MLA	mandated lead arranger
OECD	Organisation for Economic Co-operation and Development
PPP	public–private partnership
SPV	special purpose vehicle

EXECUTIVE SUMMARY

The objective of this report is to understand the current infrastructure finance scenario in the post-coronavirus disease (COVID-19) pandemic era and to explore options that can expand the availability of debt finance for infrastructure projects in Southeast Asia. Given that the pandemic has resulted in a broader global downturn, the study is motivated by the key role expected from the infrastructure sector in leading Asian economies toward recovery.

While the global need for substantial infrastructure and contribution to sustainable development was well recognized before COVID-19, quality and more resilient infrastructure has come under greater focus as societies face strained health systems, disruption in supply chains, increasing unemployment, deflationary pressures in energy markets, and disruption in transportation. In this context, the immediate growth driver from infrastructure investment is through construction. The Global Infrastructure Hub estimates that the short-term fiscal growth multiplier, on average, reached 0.80 within 1 year, and 1.53 within 2–5 years. These multipliers from public infrastructure investment are significantly higher than from spending on social transfers, where the 2–5 year multiplier was estimated at 0.84.

Globally, in 2020, the gross domestic product (GDP) fell to –3.3%, the labor market shrunk by 114 million jobs, and international investment declined by around 42% to an estimated $859 billion. According to a study by the Asian Development Bank (ADB), about 27%–30% of the global losses accrued to developing Asian economies, where the drop in regional GDP is estimated at $1.4 trillion to $2.2 trillion for 2020. Compared to developing Asia, losses in the United States were slightly smaller, while losses in Europe were larger as a share of GDP.

Role of infrastructure investment in post-pandemic recovery

While COVID-19 delivered a blow to developing Asian economies, it also highlighted the importance of investing in infrastructure to improve resilience. Current projections still point to sustained increases in infrastructure investments in global emerging markets, with developing Asia as the key region where most new infrastructure will be built. The region will invest $1.7 trillion annually over the next 20 years, up from $1 trillion during 2007–2018. The People's Republic of China will remain the largest contributor, while India will be the second largest to contribute 10% of developing Asia spending. However, governments can only cover 37% of total target spending in the next 5 years.

While historically infrastructure has been owned by the public and financed through taxation and public debt, private capital has come to play an increasing role in infrastructure development. The need to complement public investment and attract private capital to infrastructure is particularly salient in the context of the post-pandemic recovery, with governments facing unprecedented levels of debt due to extraordinary fiscal policies. Public–private partnerships can prove useful to deliver infrastructure and accelerate long-term economic recovery by matching public and private money, and they are regarded as the preferred method for infrastructure delivery in emerging Asian economies.

Alternative investment and risk-sharing models

Debt fund model. Infrastructure debt funds are relatively new players in the field of project finance. These funds are investment vehicles that provide debt to infrastructure projects under the form of direct loans and, to a lesser extent, bonds. The debt fund model is probably the easiest way to approach the infrastructure market for institutional investors, even for the less sophisticated ones and those without a specific, dedicated team to invest in relative assets. With this model, investors make an unfunded commitment to the limited partnership, which is drawn during the term of the fund that is raised and managed by investment professionals who screen, analyze, invest, monitor, and implement value creation actions in infrastructure projects. The strategic asset allocation is defined from the outset of the deal, which allows institutional investors to select the fund that best suits their investment needs, for instance, achieving a risk diversification advantage. The success of the debt fund model is contingent on a strong deal flow.

Direct lending model. With direct lending, institutional investors invest in infrastructure loans, which can be either originated by a mandated lead arranger (MLA) bank in a partnership or co-investment, or with a direct origination of infrastructure loans by institutional investors themselves. In the partnership or co-investment approach, an institutional investor invests in infrastructure loans originated by an MLA bank and participates in a syndication process and the MLA bank retains a pre-agreed percentage of each loan in its portfolio. Between 2010 and 2018, many banks entered into partnership agreements with institutional investors. Partnerships present advantages, both from the point of view of banks and institutional investors. A partnership creates a captive market for funding and banks can secure funding for infrastructure from partner institutional investors.

Securitization. A securitization transaction involves repackaging the risk of a portfolio of financial assets. This risk is passed on to a special purpose vehicle (SPV), either by transferring the portfolio to the SPV (cash securitization) or using credit derivative techniques (synthetic securitization, when risk is transferred through bundled loans via credit derivatives or guarantees). The risk is then sold to the capital markets by way of securities issued by the SPV. These securities are rated by credit rating agencies according to their seniority within the capital structure. A broad range of investor groups purchase the securities based on their individual risk/return preferences and investment criteria. An asset manager typically manages the underlying pool of loans by constructing a portfolio and optimizing portfolio performance. Investors in the securities bear the risk of losses suffered by the portfolio. The whole transaction benefits from this scheme because the credit strength of the notes will generally be stronger than the credit strength of any individual project loan, as pooled cash flows diversify default risk.

INTRODUCTION

The objective of this report is to understand the current infrastructure finance scenario in the post-coronavirus disease (COVID-19) pandemic era and to explore options that can expand the availability of finance for infrastructure projects, with regard to debt financing, in Southeast Asia. Given that the pandemic has resulted in a broader global downturn, the study is motivated by the key role expected from the infrastructure sector in leading Asian economies toward recovery.[1]

Even if the global need for substantial infrastructure and their contribution to sustainable development was widely recognized well before COVID-19, in the wake of the pandemic, quality and more resilient infrastructure has come under greater focus as societies face strained health systems, disruption in supply chains, increasing unemployment, deflationary pressures in energy markets, and disruption in transportation. In this context, the immediate growth driver from infrastructure investment is through construction. The Global Infrastructure Hub estimates that the short-term fiscal multiplier, on average, reached 0.80 within 1 year, and 1.53 within 2–5 years.[2] The estimates also show that the multiplier effect from public infrastructure investment is significantly higher than from alternative spending such as social transfers, where the 2–5 year multiplier was estimated at 0.84. In the medium to long term, infrastructure plays an increasingly pivotal role in the achievement of the United Nations Sustainable Development Goals and in the relaunch of the economies through spending in renewable energies and decarbonization policies.

While historically a substantial proportion of infrastructure has been owned by the public authorities and financed through taxation and/or public debt, over the last 30 years private capital has played an increasing role in the financing and development of infrastructure. The need to complement public investment and attract private capital to infrastructure is particularly salient in the context of the post-pandemic recovery, with governments facing unprecedented levels of debt due to extraordinary fiscal policies. Public–private partnerships (PPPs), which allow for headline measures of government indebtedness to be unaffected, can prove useful to deliver infrastructure and accelerate long-term economic recovery by matching public and private money, and they are regarded as the preferred method for infrastructure delivery in emerging Asian economies.

In this context, to attract more private finance to the infrastructure sector, governments and multilateral development banks (MDBs) can introduce policies and financial instruments to mitigate the financial risks associated with infrastructure development. Given the prominent role of MDBs in fostering infrastructure development, in 2015 the Group of Twenty (G20) endorsed the MDB Action Plan to Optimize Balance Sheets,[3] which proposed a range of techniques to expand lending by attracting a broader class of private institutional investors. In more recent years, as the availability of debt capital for infrastructure has further diminished in the context of Basel III capital adequacy and capital requirements, as well as in the wake of the COVID-19 pandemic, forms of cooperation between banks and institutional investors, as well as policy instruments, are indispensable elements

---

[1]   International Monetary Fund (IMF) World Economic Outlook April 2021.Since the onset of COVID-19 lockdowns in the second quarter (Q2) of 2020, global private infrastructure investment has been trending downward. In the fourth quarter (Q4) of 2020, private infrastructure investment was just 60% of the level in Q4 2019.

[2]   Global Infrastructure Hub. 2020. Fiscal multiplier effect of infrastructure investment.

[3]   G20. 2015. Multilateral Development Banks Action Plan to Optimize Balance Sheets.

to attract long-term investors to the infrastructure sector. The aim of this report is to present these forms of cooperation, including co-investment, risk-sharing and risk-shifting techniques, and policy instruments that support private lending to infrastructure projects, as well as examples of project applications to support a faster deployment by governments and MDBs globally. While these forms of cooperation were introduced well before COVID-19, the report claims that their role will be more prominent to attract long-term investors to the infrastructure sector in the context of the post-pandemic recovery. In fact, COVID-19 has represented a catalyst for some of the trends that are discussed and analyzed in the following sections of the report.

The report is organized as follows: Section 2 analyzes the effects of the COVID-19 pandemic on the economy, both globally and in Asia, highlighting how infrastructure investment is becoming a growing challenge as governments face unprecedented levels of debt and banks are prudently reducing credit commitments in view of a rebound in corporate defaults. Section 3 discusses the salient role of infrastructure in stimulating economies for a sustainable economic recovery in Asia in the post-COVID-19 scenario, while Section 4 reviews the current trends and challenges in infrastructure finance. As traditional sources of infrastructure funding from governments and banks would not be sufficient to address the demand for infrastructure financing, Section 5 presents three main forms of cooperation between banks and institutional investors that expand lending to infrastructure: the debt fund model, the direct lending model, and the securitization model. Section 6 discusses approaches under which governments and MDBs can enhance the risk profile of infrastructure investments and improve its attractiveness for the private sector. Section 7 concludes and summarizes the key policy implications.

THE IMPACT OF COVID-19 ON THE GLOBAL ECONOMY

The COVID-19 pandemic has taken a toll on the global economy. As of the beginning of September 2022, the World Health Organization reported 613.94 million COVID-19 infections and 6.5 million deaths, with Asia accounting for 18% of cases and 14% of deaths.[4] The globalized world and interconnectedness facilitated the rapid spread and impact of the pandemic. Throughout the crisis, governments adopted extraordinary policies aimed at containing the spread of the virus. This led to a collapse in global demand and supply. However, the impact differed across sectors in line with their vulnerability to the containment measures.

Globally, in 2020, the gross domestic product (GDP) fell to −3.3%,[5] the labor market shrunk by 114 million jobs,[6] and international investment declined by around 42% to an estimated $859 billion.[7] According to a study by the Asian Development Bank (ADB),[8] about 27%–30% of the global losses accrued to developing Asian economies, where the drop in regional GDP is estimated at $1.4 trillion to $2.2 trillion for 2020. Compared to developing Asia, losses in the United States were slightly smaller, while losses in Europe were larger as a share of GDP. A more in-depth analysis of the impact of COVID-19 on the Asian economy is included in Box 1.

Box 1: The Impact of COVID-19 on Asian Economies

Impact on growth

As per gross domestic product (GDP) growth estimates for 2020 and forecasts for 2021 of the Asian Development Bank, developing Asia recorded a −0.2% GDP real growth in 2020 and is estimated to rebound to 4.6% in 2022 and 5.2% in 2023.[a] With regard specifically to Southeast Asia, major economies including Indonesia, Malaysia, the Philippines, and Thailand recorded significant negative growth rates.[b] For Asian economies that had particularly severe second quarter (Q2) 2020 downturns and prolonged lockdowns, estimates of the 2020 impact on consumption and investment are larger. Thus, in India and the Philippines, 2020 consumption is expected to be 12%–15% lower and investment about 25% lower than pre-coronavirus disease (COVID-19) expectations. These new estimates are twice as large as they were in June 2020. Other economies also witnessed downward revisions to 2020 consumption, including Hong Kong, China; Malaysia; and Singapore. However, there was a more even split between downward and upward revisions to 2020 investment, as some economies including the People's Republic of China (PRC); the Republic of Korea; and Taipei,China rebounded more rapidly.[c] The impact of COVID-19 on growth in developing and emerging Asia is provided in the table.

(continued on next page)

---

4   World Health Organization. Coronavirus dashboard (accessed 30 September 2022).
5   IMF. World Economic Outlook (April 2021).
6   International Labour Organization. World Employment and Social Outlook (June 2021).
7   United Nations Conference on Trade and Development (UNCTAD). Impact of the COVID-19 pandemic on trade and development (March 2021).
8   Y. Sawada and L. R. Sumulong. 2021. Macroeconomic Impact of COVID-19 in Developing Asia. *ADBI Working Paper Series.* No. 1251. Tokyo: Asian Development Bank Institute.

Box 1 *(continued)*

Table: GDP Growth Estimates and Projections for Emerging and Developing Asia
(%)

| | Estimates | | Projections | | Q4 over Q4 | | |
| | | | | | Estimate | Projections | |
	2019	2020	2022	2023	2020	2022	2023
Emerging and developing Asia (total)	5.4	1.1	4.6	5.2	3.2	4.4	5.8
PRC	6.0	2.3	4.0	4.8	6.2	4.8	4.7
India	4.2	–8.0	7.2	67.8	6.2	2.7	9.0
Southeast Asia	4.9	3.7	5.0	5.2	0.6	5.1	5.3

GDP = gross domestic product, PRC = People's Republic of China, Q4 = fourth quarter.
Sources: Asian Development Outlook Supplement, July 2022 and International Monetary Fund World Economic Outlook 2022.

Even prior to the pandemic, there were concerns that rising debt levels in Asia could trigger a new crisis. Unfortunately, the health of the real and financial sectors was deteriorating. The Asian financial system was showing signs of vulnerability, with lower margins, higher risk costs, and continued dependence on banks and shadow-banking institutions, and a capital buffer that could be under stress. As of May 2020, the financial services sector in Asia had lost over $920 billion in market value, due to investor concerns about the increasingly high levels of bank nonperforming loans (NPLs) due to COVID-19.[d]

Impact on the real sector

In the real sector, corporates across the region were under stress to fulfill their debt service obligations, and households in Australia and the Republic of Korea had accumulated unsustainable levels of debt. Association of Southeast Asian Nations (ASEAN) firms do not appear to have engaged in excessive risk-taking prior to the pandemic, in contrast with the Asian financial crisis of the late 1990s. In general, firms have kept their balance sheet leverage broadly stable since the global financial crisis,[e] while gradually reducing reliance on short-term debt.[f] Further, the level of their outstanding foreign exchange debt has generally moved in parallel with their foreign sales volume, limiting the exposure to currency risks. Consequently, firms entered the pandemic with relatively more resilient balance sheets than in the past.

However, many firms had encountered the pandemic with high debt service burden, due to a sustained decline in profitability since the global financial crisis, and the rise in financing costs. In 2019, an estimated one-third of firms in the region were unable to cover their interest payments with their income earned from business operations. About a quarter were "zombie firms" (defined as firms aged 10 years or more with persistent debt service difficulties for at least the last 5 years) (footnote e). The debt service burden was particularly high among firms in energy, materials, and consumer discretionary industries; and small-sized firms.

Along with the above preexisting vulnerabilities, ASEAN firms now must cope with the pandemic. Given the large uncertainty as to the size and persistence of the COVID-19 shock across different industries, assessing the expected impact of COVID-19 is difficult. According to the International Monetary Fund (IMF) (footnote e), over 60% of firms in the energy sector and consumer discretionary sectors would generate insufficient incomes to cover interest payments for the period ending 2020. This is significantly higher than the estimated 40% of firms in the period ending 2019. Meanwhile, the liquidity buffer to sustain the COVID-19 shocks was low even for many viable firms before the pandemic. Over 50% of firms did not have enough cash holdings to cover 3 months' worth of cost of goods sold in 2019. The cash-flow-generating capacity was also weak with about a quarter of sample firms experiencing difficulties in maintaining positive operating cash flows during 2017–2019.

Box 1 *(continued)*

An overview of ASEAN firms at risk is provided in the table.

Without policy interventions, a wave of corporate bankruptcies may be possible. Close to 50% of firms may be unable to generate enough earnings to cover their interest payments. About one-third of sample firms would run out of cash without liquidity support. Across industries, the share of these high-risk firms is expected to be the highest in energy and consumer discretionary sectors, which reflects both a relatively larger than expected impact of the COVID-19 shocks and firms' already high debt service burden before the pandemic.

Impact on the financial sector

For most of 2020, profitability, cost, and solvency of the banks in ASEAN largely tracked global institutions. Net interest margin (NIM) proved resilient within the ASEAN emerging markets, although COVID-19-related stresses continued to make their way through banks with credit rating downgrades, impairment charges, and provisions in early 2021.[g] However, improved performance is expected in the event of significant reopening of the ASEAN economies in the second half of 2021. In some economies in Central Asia, East Asia, and South Asia, economies, NPL ratios have been rising. Fiscal stimulus has helped prevent corporate defaults, while regulatory forbearance has relieved pressure on banks. However, post-pandemic corporate default risks expose banks to high NPLs, with harmful macro-financial feedback effects. In addition, high NPLs also risk cross-border spillovers and contagion effects through cross-border bank networks.

Although banks remained resilient amid the COVID-19 pandemic, profits have been hit. In the Asia and Pacific region, bank profitability weakened as reflected by the drop in weighted average return on assets (ROA), from 0.82% in the first half of fiscal year 2019 to 0.66% in the same period in 2020.[h] The NIM of banks has been squeezed by the cuts in interest rates.[i]

Meanwhile, banks made larger loan-loss provisions to prepare for the potential surge in NPLs especially after the financial aid measures introduced by regulators end. In addition, some economies witnessed slower credit growth. Fitch Ratings expects further deterioration in asset quality and earnings headwinds stemming from modest growth, tight NIMs, and

Table: ASEAN +6: Firms at Risk by Industry

Percentage of firms generating inadequate earnings to cover interest payments

	End of 2019	End of 2020 (minimum)	End of 2020 (maximum)
Energy	41	57	68
Materials	39	47	67
Consumer discretionary	38	46	66
Information technology	37	41	42
Communications	37	37	41
Industrials	30	47	50
Real estate	28	47	58
Health care	27	28	37
Consumer staples	30	32	41
Utilities	19	20	40

Note: Projection as of early 2020. "ASEAN + 6" is a grouping of 16 countries comprising the 10 Association of Southeast Asian Nations (ASEAN) member countries of Brunei Darussalam, Myanmar, Cambodia, Indonesia, the Philippines, Malaysia, the Lao People's Democratic Republic, Singapore, Thailand, and Viet Nam plus Australia, India, Japan, New Zealand, the People's Republic of China, and the Republic of Korea.
Source: S&P Global Market Intelligence and IMF staff estimates.

Table: Credit Costs in Asia and Pacific Banking Systems
(% of gross loans)

	End of 2019	June 2020
Republic of Korea	0.08	0.22
Indonesia	0.80	2.00
India	3.50	2.35
Philippines	0.41	2.38
Thailand	1.35	1.85
PRC	1.20	1.46
Viet Nam	0.74	1.34
Malaysia	0.31	0.93

PRC = People's Republic of China.
Source: Fitch Ratings, Special Report Credit Costs in Asia and Pacific 2021.

Box 1 (*continued*)

elevated credit and operating costs.[j] Annualized credit costs across 79 of the largest Fitch Ratings-rated banks in the Asia and Pacific region increased to an average of 1.26% of gross loans in the first half of 2020, from 0.84% in 2019, as shown in the next table. The rise was more pronounced in emerging Asian markets. This may reflect policy responses and relative impact of the pandemic shocks, as well as bank risk management measures.

Table: COVID-19 Impact on Credit Losses and Nonperforming Assets

	2018 (actual)		2019 (actual)		2020 (forecast)		2021 (forecast)	
	Credit losses	NPAs	Credit losses	NPAs	Credit losses	NPAs	Credit losses	NPAs
Republic of Korea	0.25	1.0	0.20	1.0	0.25	1.9	0.50	1.7
Indonesia	1.25	2.2	1.75	2.3	2.8	3.5	2.7	4.0
India	3.1	9.0	2.9	8.4	3.0	10.1	2.8	10.3
Philippines	0.4	3.5	0.5	3.6	1.6	5.5	1.45	7.5
Thailand	1.2	3.5	1.3	3.4	2.0	4.9	1.7	6.0
PRC	1.5	2.0	1.35	4.8	2.2	8.2	1.6	7.9
Viet Nam	0.7	2.1	0.7	1.8	1.85	5.1	1.8	6.9
Malaysia	0.1	1.8	0.05	1.7	0.7	5.0	0.6	6.9

COVID-19 = coronavirus disease, NPA= nonperforming asset, PRC = People's Republic of China.
Credit losses are net charge-offs of private sector exposures or loan-loss provisions allocated to cover potential losses on exposures to resident borrowers by resident banks, and are expressed as a percentage of the average of loans to domestic borrowers. Nonperforming assets are the sum of problematic exposures (including loans and foreclosed assets) due by resident borrowers to a country's resident banks as a percentage of loans granted to private and public borrowers.
Source: S&P Global Banks Outlook: November 2020.

COVID-19 hit lenders and bank credit losses were expected to rise by about $500 billion by year-end 2021. Standard & Poor's took negative rating actions on banks since the onset of COVID-19, including in Australia, Japan, India, Indonesia, Malaysia, New Zealand, the Philippines, and Thailand. A more severe or prolonged hit to the economies is the main downside risk, as the damage on households and corporates would intensify credit losses and drive earnings down. In many countries, banks have high exposure to the property sector, and prices and private sector debt remain high. This could trigger a disorderly correction in asset prices, which would heighten and prolong banks' asset quality problems. As a consequence, the pandemic is also expected to push up credit losses and nonperforming assets, as shown in the table above.

The next table compares the performance of banks before and after the pandemic in selected Asian economies. In the region, Indonesia saw the largest drop in ROA. On average, the 23 Indonesian banks in the Asian Banker 500 ranking reported a 22.1% year-on-year contraction in net profit in the first half of 2020, compared to a 13.5% increase over the same period a year earlier. Average ROA fell from 2% in the first half of 2019 to 1.4% in the same period of 2020. In addition to the narrowed margins and rising loan-loss provisions, weaker lending growth also contributed to the fall in ROA.[k] During COVID-19, Japanese banks offered more loans to smaller businesses hit by the pandemic, while increasing loan-loss provisions. The average ROA of banks in Thailand and the Philippines also fell considerably. Several large Thai banks recorded lower average ROA at 0.85% in the first half of 2020, compared to 1.29% in the same period of 2019, while the average ROA of 10 banks from the Philippines fell from 1.22% to 0.8%.[l]

Box 1 (*continued*)

Table: Comparative Bank Performance Before and After Pandemic

% Change	Republic of Korea	Indonesia	India	Philippines	Thailand	PRC	Viet Nam	Malaysia
Loan Growth (2019-2020)	-0.70	-1.60	- 0.70	- 0.50	1.30	0.60	0	0.80
NIM (2019-2020)	- 12.80	3.50	-0.80	4.0	- 9.20	- 0.20	- 0.80	1.90
ROA (2016-2020)	0.50	-0.75	1.75	-0.25	-0.75	-0.25	0.50	-0.25

NIM = net interest margin, PRC = People's Republic of China, ROA = return on assets.

[a] ADB. 2021. *Asian Development Outlook (ADO) April 2021*. Financing a Green and Inclusive Recovery. Manila

[b] As per the April 2021 ADO, the Philippines (–9.6%), Malaysia (–5.6%), Thailand (–6.1%), and Indonesia (–2.1%), recorded significant contractions.

[c] ADB. 2020. The Impact of COVID-19 on Developing Asia: The Pandemic Extends into 2021. *ADB Briefs*. No. 128. Manila.

[d] McKinsey & Company. 2020. How healthy is the Asian financial system?

[e] *The Economist Intelligence Unit*. 2019. The critical role of infrastructure for the Sustainable Development Goals.

[f] C. Y. Rhee and K. Svirydzenka, eds. 2021. Policy Advice to Asia in the COVID-19 Era. *IMF Departmental Paper*. No. 2021/004. 5 March.

[g] McKinsey & Company. 2019. Signs of Stress: Is Asia Heading toward a Debt Crisis?

[h] Based on an evaluation of the top 500 largest banks in Asia and Pacific. The Asian Banker 500 (AB500).

[i] Policy rates are approaching zero for the first time in Australia, New Zealand, the Republic of Korea, and Thailand, joining other Asia and Pacific markets, such as Hong Kong, China; Japan; and Singapore, which have previous experience with ultra-low rates.

[j] Fitch Ratings 2021 Outlook: Asia-Pacific Developed Market Banks.

[k] The average loan growth of these banks decelerated significantly from 14.3% year-on-year (YoY) at the end of June 2019 to a mere 0.2% YoY at the end of June 2020. Loan demand was weak as business activity and consumer spending were stunted amid the pandemic.

[l] Bangkok Bank and Kasikornbank, the two largest Thai banks by total assets, saw net profit plummet by 41% YoY and 49% YoY, respectively, in the first half (1H) of 2020, driven by shrinking margins, lower non-interest income and higher loan-loss provisions. This does not mean that despite a general decline in net profit, some banks achieved good pre-provision earnings. For instance, the net profit of DBS in Singapore slid by 26% YoY in 1H 2020, but its pre-provision operating profit was up 12% YoY. In 1H 2020, the provisions DBS set aside against potential bad loans quintupled to $1.4 billion. BDO Unibank, the largest bank in the Philippines, recorded an 18.4% YoY increase in its pre-provision operating profit. The provisions in 1H 2020 was 7.5 times higher than that in 1H 2019, and it registered a 79% YoY plunge in its net profit.

Sources: International Monetary Fund, Financial Soundness Indicators; and Asian Development Bank estimates using data from S&P Global Market Intelligence.

In the real economy, policy makers, along with tight measures to tame the COVID-19 pandemic, implemented unprecedented fiscal and monetary measures to offset interruptions to income, credit, and spending patterns in businesses and households, and to face the health expenditures. On an overall basis, economies have been able to withstand the impact of the pandemic and avoid a total collapse due to these extraordinary policy measures, avoiding a contagion effect on the financial sector. However, the challenges on public finances continue, as shown in Figure 1.

Figure 1: Interest Expense and Government Debt, 2007–2021

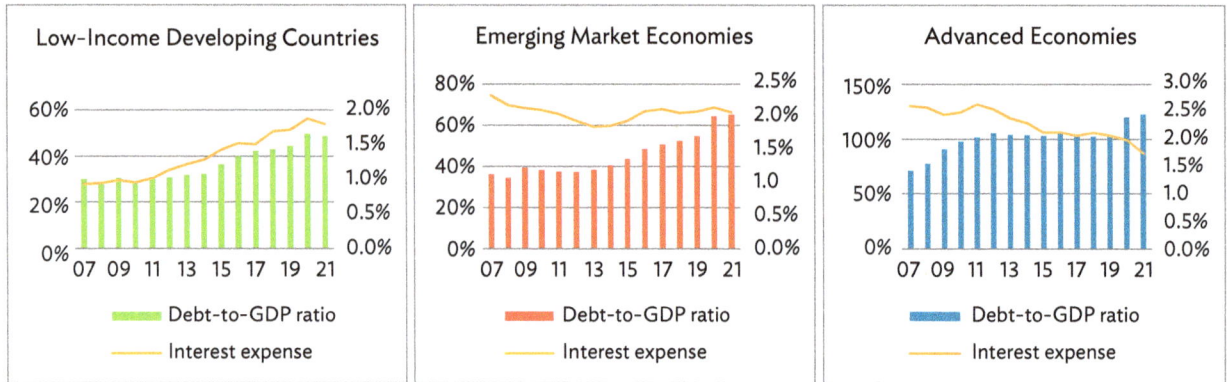

GDP = gross domestic product.
Source: International Monetary Fund. Fiscal Monitor (April 2021).

While contraction in output (i.e., GDP) and the subsequent fall (or postponement) in tax revenues widened government deficits beyond levels recorded during the global financial crisis (GFC), the fiscal response of governments was sustained with central banks reducing policy rates and expanding asset purchases. Along with banks, which are facing the global recession with higher capital and liquidity buffers after the Basel III reforms, corporates are also emerging from the pandemic with higher debt. The extraordinary drop in cost of equity and debt determined by accommodative monetary policies have helped even sub-investment grade firms raise funds. Debt and equity issuance has risen as companies tried to cope with liquidity pressures (Figure 2).

Figure 2: Global High-Yield Bond and Equity Issuance, 2007–January 2021
($ billion)

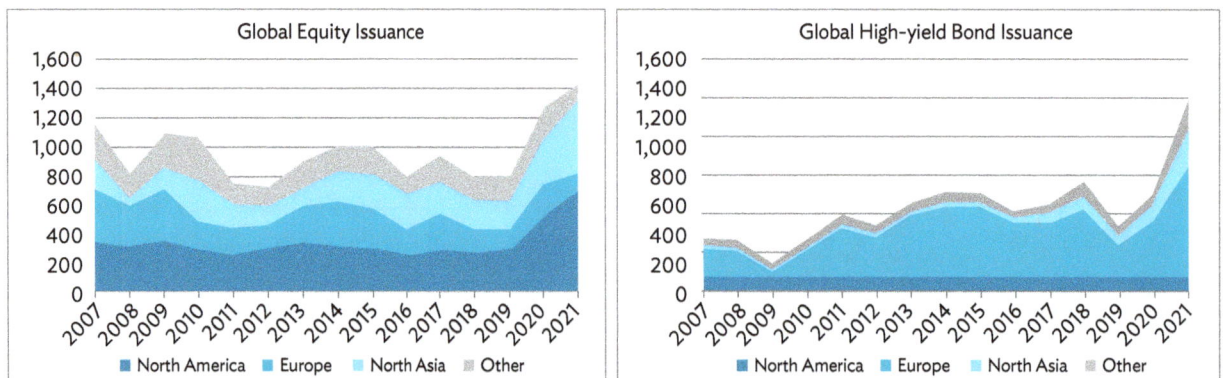

Source: International Monetary Fund. Global Financial Stability Report (April 2021).

While defaults are dropping, from GFC peaks, the growing debt, along with slow earning expectations, can impair the debt servicing capacity of pandemic-affected companies. The increase in global speculative-grade corporate defaults by sector between 2019 and 2020 is shown in Figure 3. Further, potential expiration of loan moratoria and government loan guarantees may trigger defaults, causing a deterioration in bank asset quality and a reduction in capital ratios.

Figure 3: Number of Global Speculative-Grade Corporate Defaults by Sector, 2019–2020

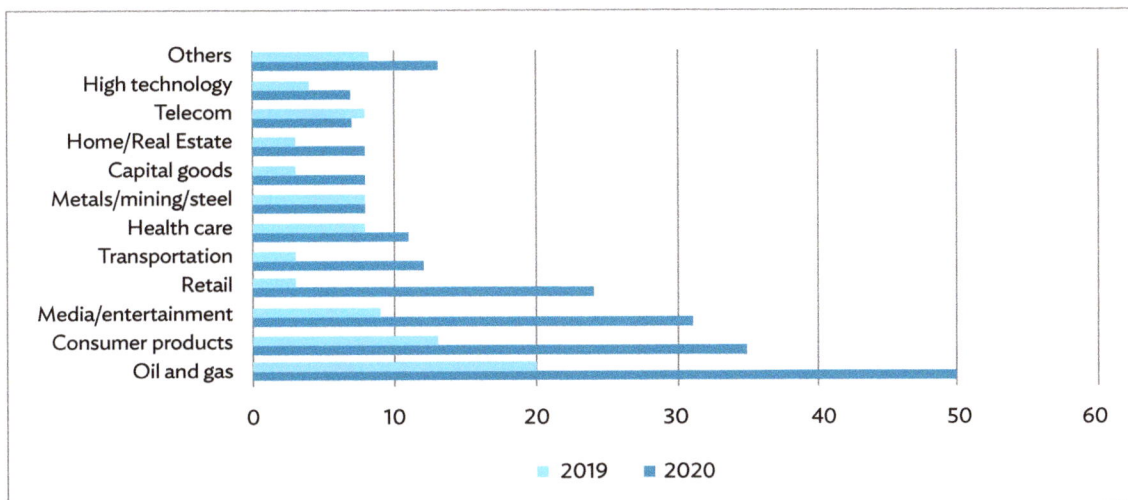

Source: International Monetary Fund. Global Financial Stability Report (April 2021).

Against this backdrop, expectations for a global recovery were earlier optimistic, sustained by the increasing availability of vaccines, and extended macroeconomic policy support. The Organisation for Economic Co-operation and Development (OECD) estimated a rebound of global GDP growth of 5.8% in 2021.[9] However, the Asian Development Outlook Supplement of July 2022 revised the growth forecasts for developing Asia from 5.2% to 4.6% for 2022 and from 5.3% to 5.2% for 2023, reflecting worsened economic prospects in the wake of the Russian invasion of Ukraine, more aggressive monetary tightening in advanced economies, and continued COVID-19 lockdowns in the People's Republic of China.[10] The revisions also reflect variations in pandemic-induced impacts; the extent of policy measures; and the pace of vaccinations leading to diverging recoveries across countries and sectors, especially in developing- and emerging-market regions.

In this scenario, given the need for global economies to recover a stable path of growth, it is widely recognized that investments should be addressed to strengthen the infrastructure stock. With particular reference to Asia, while COVID-19 delivered a heavy blow to developing Asian economies and the recovery of some markets will be protracted (Box 1), it also highlighted the importance of investing in infrastructure to improve resilience in the region.[11] As we discuss in the following section, infrastructure plays a direct role in stimulating economies and maintaining employment, and represents a key sector for the regional economic recovery in the post-COVID-19 scenario. However, financing infrastructure investment is becoming a growing challenge for many

---

[9]   OECD Economic Outlook (May 2021).
[10] ADB. 2022. *Asian Development Outlook (ADO) 2022 Supplement: Recovery Faces Diverse Challenges*. Manila.
[11] Asian Infrastructure Investment Bank. 2020. *Asian infrastructure finance 2020: Investing Better, Investing More.*

Asian economies as public finance is under pressure as a result of COVID-19-induced economic recession. At the same time, the banking sector is primarily focusing on corporate lending under public credit enhancement programs and concerned with resulting liquidity and solvency risks, reducing its exposures to the infrastructure sector. In this context, attracting long-term institutional investors such as pension funds and insurers is key to fill the infrastructure gap and sustain the region's economic recovery.

THE SALIENT ROLE OF INFRASTRUCTURE IN A SUSTAINABLE POST-PANDEMIC RECOVERY

3

The global need for substantial infrastructure and their contribution to economic development was widely recognized well before COVID-19. The OECD estimates global infrastructure investment needs of $6.3 trillion per year over the period 2016–2030 to support growth and equal development.[12] ADB estimates around $1.7 trillion would have to be invested annually in infrastructure across Asia until 2030 to sustain economic progress, eradicate poverty, and respond effectively to climate change.[13] An analysis of infrastructure needs and challenges in Asia can be found in Box 2.

Box 2: Infrastructure Needs in Asia

A fast-growing, rapidly urbanizing population has driven demand for infrastructure in emerging markets, where investments in this sector have grown considerably in recent years. Overall, infrastructure investments increased by 4.7% per annum in global emerging markets during 2007–2018, compared to just 1% per annum in advanced markets.[a] Developing Asia accounted for 75% of total emerging markets and 45% of global spend on infrastructure during the period. This was mainly driven by the People's Republic of China (PRC), whose infrastructure investment grew by an annual average of 6.2% to account for about two-thirds of the emerging Asia total during the decade. India also reported strong increases by an annual rate of 7%, though its share of emerging Asia total remains small at 8%. The relative share of other key emerging markets in Asia varies from 3.2% for Indonesia to around 1% each for Thailand, Malaysia, Viet Nam, and the Philippines. It is also important to note that while the PRC invested around 7% of its gross domestic product (GDP) and Viet Nam invested 5.7% of its GDP in infrastructure, the rest of the key emerging Asian markets invested in the range of 3%–4% of their GDP. The figure shows the average growth rate of infrastructure investments and their share to GDP in selected developing Asian economies.

In the wake of the pandemic, the stringent lockdowns and social distancing norms due to the coronavirus disease (COVID-19) have severely disrupted the construction industry across South Asia and Southeast Asia. Consequently, construction was expected to contract by 8.5% in 2020 in the region. India's second COVID-19 wave affected its infrastructure sectors to varying degrees, with power companies and ports better able to weather the impact of pandemic-induced disruptions compared to airports and toll roads.[b] The slump in the output is reflected in the unprecedented sharp contraction in infrastructure investment in the second quarter of 2020 in Singapore (59.3%), India (50.3%), Malaysia (44.5%), and the Philippines (33.5%).[c]

(continued on next page)

---

[12] M. Mirabile, V. Marchal, and R. Baron. 2017. *Technical note on estimates of infrastructure investment needs*. OECD.
[13] ADB. 2017. *Meeting Asia's Infrastructure Needs*. Manila.

Box 2 *(continued)*

Figure: Infrastructure Investment, 2007–2018

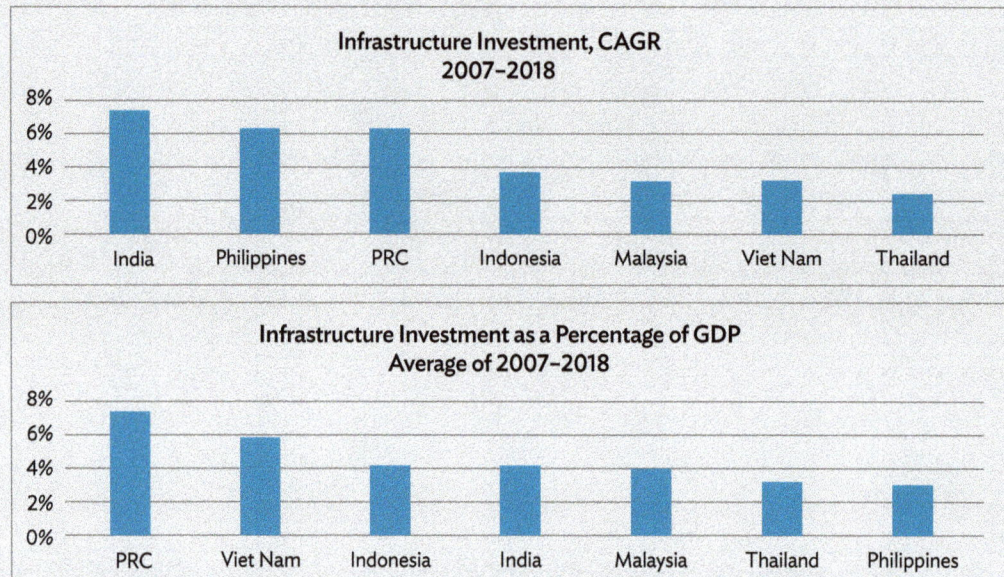

CAGR = compound annual growth rate, GDP = gross domestic product, PRC = People's Republic of China.
Source: Infrastructure investment numbers are estimated using the "infrastructure investment as percent of GDP" data from the Global Infrastructure Outlook by the Global Infrastructure Hub and Oxford Economics, gross fixed capital formation data from the World Bank, and GDP estimates and forecasts from Swiss Re Institute.

While COVID-19 delivered a heavy blow to developing Asian economies, it also highlighted the importance of investing in infrastructure to improve resilience. Current projections are still pointing to sustained increases in infrastructure investments in global emerging markets, with developing Asia as the key region where most new infrastructure will be built. The region will invest $1.7 trillion annually over the next 20 years, up from $1 trillion spend during 2007–2018.[d] The PRC will remain the largest contributor, while India will be the second largest to contribute 10% of developing Asia spending. Sector-wise, road (35% of total investment) and energy (34%) will be the key infrastructure growth sectors in emerging Asia over the next 20 years. Around one-third of the energy investment will be in renewable sources, mainly driven by the PRC and India. Current share of renewables in power capacity stands at 11% in Indonesia, 22% in Malaysia, and 22% in Thailand, compared with an Asia average of 34%, leaving ample room for investment and expansion.[d] Government can only cover 37% of total target spending in the next 5 years (footnote c).

[a] Swiss Re Group. 2020. Post-COVID recovery: Infrastructure in Emerging Asia holds the key. 19 October.
[b] Moody's Investors Service 2021.
[c] OECD. 2021. Insurance Statistics 2020.
[d] McKinsey & Company. 2020. Reimagining emerging ASEAN in the wake of COVID-19.

In the wake of the pandemic, quality and more resilient infrastructure has come under greater focus as societies face strained health systems, disruption in supply chains, increasing unemployment, deflationary pressures in energy markets, and disruption in transportation.[14] In the short term, increased expenditure on infrastructure will have an immediate effect by boosting employment and supporting economic growth through spending on construction activity. In a recent analysis, the Global Infrastructure Hub showed that the short-term fiscal multiplier of infrastructure investments, on average, reached 0.80 within 1 year, and 1.53 within 2–5 years (footnote 3). In the medium to long term, infrastructure will play an increasingly pivotal role for the achievement of the United Nations Sustainable Development Goals and in the relaunch of economies through spending in renewable energy and decarbonization policies.[15]

However, the fallout of the COVID-19 crisis had a serious impact on infrastructure and related assets; in 2020, the asset class as a whole witnessed an unusual negative return of –3.3%. Construction has been suspended or postponed due to absence of workers, supply chain disruptions, delayed or canceled tenders, lower demand forecasts, and the reallocation of government funds. In multiple sectors, user-fee-dependent operational assets faced a significant decrease in demand and increased project risks by way of debt sustainability, defaults, termination, insolvency, or government breaching of contracts.[16]

Different infrastructure sectors were affected to a different extent by the pandemic, specifically according to their exposure to demand risk in service provision, as shown in Figure 4. Demand-based assets such as in airports, ports, and toll roads were particularly impacted by the drop of demand by end users. Aeronautical revenues pertaining to landing charges for aircraft and security charges fell as airport capacity was slashed. Non-aeronautical revenues, derived from airports' parking facilities, restaurants, or duty free, also plummeted as the volume of travelers was minimized. According to the Airport Council International, COVID-19 triggered an estimated 66.3% reduction in airport revenues, reducing them from a forecast baseline of $188 billion to close to $125 billion in 2020.[17] In the power sector, lockdown measures significantly reduced electricity consumption in the commercial and manufacturing sectors, but increased residential demand. According to the International Energy Agency, while global electricity consumption fell by 4% in 2020, the drop in demand did not affect all fuels equally.[18] Oil was the hardest hit, as restrictions on mobility caused demand for transport fuels to fall by 14% in 2020 compared to 2019. However, renewables grew by 3% in 2020 due to new capacity and priority market access.

For utility networks, regulated assets proved resilient to the pandemic-induced volatility, mainly due to the protection of their cash flows granted by regulations or long-term contracts. For example, to compensate for the loss of revenue, urban transport, power, and water companies were offered liquidity lines or income support by public authorities, indicating that availability-based activities, although at risk from reduced or reallocated government budgets, are more resilient. In sharp contrast, the telecommunications sector was generally exempted from COVID-19 restrictions as it was recognized as an essential service. Multiple industry players—from broadband to mobile to data center operators—have benefited from a surge in data traffic.[19] Nonetheless, the digital divide within

---

[14]   OECD. 2021. *COVID-19 and a new resilient infrastructure landscape*. 22 February.
[15]   *The Economist Intelligence Unit*. 2019. The critical role of infrastructure for the Sustainable Development Goals.
[16]   World Bank. 2020. *Infrastructure financing in times of COVID-19: A driver for recovery?* 24 July.
[17]   Airport Council International. 2021. *The impact of COVID-19 on the airport business and the path to recovery*. 25 March.
[18]   International Energy Agency. 2021. *Global energy review 2021*.
[19]   International Telecommunication Union. 2020. Economic impact of COVID-19 on digital infrastructure.

Figure 4: Estimates of Revenue Change for Listed Infrastructure, 2020–2021

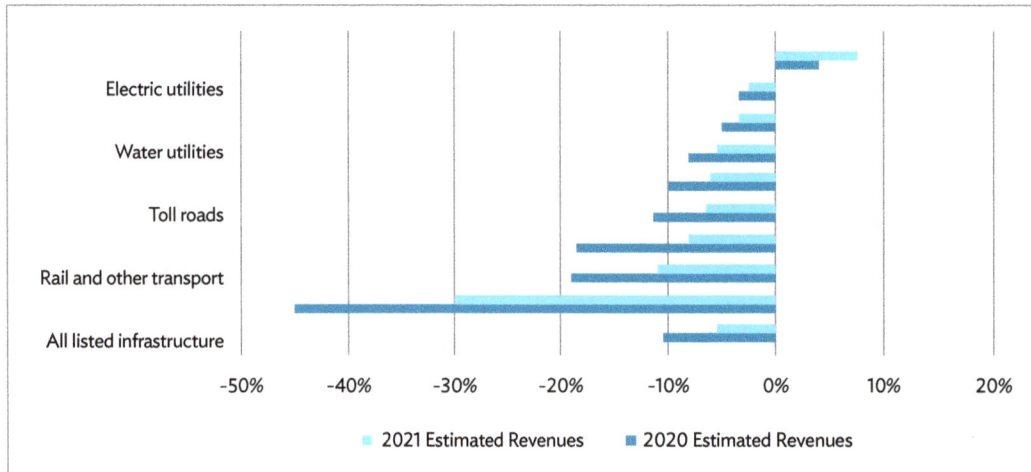

Source: UBS Asset Management (December 2020).

nations and between advanced and developing economies was exposed by the pandemic as it exacerbated the disadvantage of unserved populations, limiting access to payments and commerce, health-care services and information, and education supply.[20]

While the pandemic has brought to the surface weaknesses regarding the construction and the operational resiliency of infrastructure with the asset class witnessing a negative return in 2020, over the longer term unlisted infrastructure is delivering annualized return of around 8%–9%, second only to private equity over 3–5 years (footnote 20). After a historic low in 2020, investment levels in infrastructure are partially returning to pre-pandemic levels in many countries, indicating that the infrastructure business is slowly adopting to a new normal amid the pandemic. However, in the post-pandemic era, promoting the adequacy and resilience of infrastructure throughout the entire project life cycle appears even more critical to sustain the economic and societal development in the medium to long term. Infrastructure investments lie at the heart of the packages that governments are currently preparing to stimulate economic recovery and address the challenges of the post-COVID-19 era.[21] In particular, countries are investing in green infrastructure to spur economic recovery and create jobs. The European Union, for example, unveiled the Fit-for-55 package under the Next Generation EU recovery fund on Green Deal objectives, a €750 billion COVID-19 relief package that includes boosting clean energy and transport, with the goal of carbon neutrality by 2050.[22] Likewise, the People's Republic of China has announced an intent to attract $500 billion in new infrastructure investment, including electric vehicle charging stations.

Current investment decisions on infrastructure spending will impact the competitiveness of economies and determine their performance toward economic, social, and environmental targets. To this end, in 2019 the G20, recognizing that "the world still faces a massive gap in financing for investment in new and existing infrastructure, which could generate a serious bottleneck to

---

[20]   Preqin Quarterly Update: Infrastructure Q1 2021 (April 2021).
[21]   OECD. 2020. G20/OECD Report on the Collaboration with Institutional Investors and Asset Managers on Infrastructure.
[22]   European Parliament. Legislative Train Schedule. Fit for 55 Package Under The European Green Deal.

economic growth and development or provision of secure and reliable public services" in order to mobilize private capital and "develop infrastructure as an asset class, and maximising the positive impact of infrastructure investment," endorsed a set of principles for promoting not only quantity, but also quality of infrastructure investment. Such principles are as follows:[23]

(i)   Maximizing the positive impact of infrastructure to achieve sustainable growth and development.

(ii)   Raising economic efficiency in view of life cycle costs.

(iii)   Integrating environmental considerations in infrastructure investments.

(iv)   Building resilience against natural hazards and other risks.

(v)   Integrating social considerations in infrastructure investments.

(vi)   Strengthening infrastructure governance.

In this context, more than ever, given the high demand for sustainable infrastructure and the limits to government investment spending, attracting long-term private investors such as pension funds and life insurance companies is essential to close the infrastructure gap and move infrastructure investment forward.

---

[23]   G20 Principles for Quality Infrastructure Investment.

4

TRENDS IN PRIVATE INFRASTRUCTURE FINANCING

While the demand for infrastructure is high to sustain the post-COVID-19 recovery, many governments are facing severe fiscal constraints as a result of the significant resources that have been spent on trying to mitigate the substantial economic and social impacts of the pandemic. These constraints mean that governments will have to increasingly rely on private investment to help finance infrastructure development.

Total private investment in infrastructure has increased over the past decades, both in the form of debt and equity, and there are different vehicles on offer for private investment in infrastructure, both listed and unlisted.[24] Despite the increasing appeal of infrastructure, there is still a lot of uncertainty among private investors given the unclear global macroeconomic outlook. For this reason, infrastructure investment recorded a historic 52% drop in private participation in 2020, compared to 2019 levels.[25] Even if private investment commitments in 2021 marked an increase of 68% from 2020, they are still lower by 12% compared to the previous 5-year average (2016–2020).[26] In addition, there has been a notable shift in investment toward markets that are considered safer by investors and countries that have had more success in combating the pandemic. Concerns about political and regulatory risks, inflation and currency risks, credit quality, liquidity of borrowers, and financial robustness of counterparties, especially in developing countries, continue to linger (Box 3). The following paragraphs discuss the most recent market trends in private infrastructure financing on both the debt and equity side.

Box 3: The Risks to Investing in Infrastructure in Developing Markets

As the demand for infrastructure continues to rise, many developing countries are struggling to address their infrastructure needs, and the volume of private participation in financing infrastructure projects in these markets remains modest in comparison with developed countries. According to a survey by Probitas Partners, 71% of institutional investors are less interested in investing in developing markets due to high political, counterparty or sovereign, or currency risk.[a]

In addition to risks specific to the infrastructure sector, the Organisation for Economic Co-operation and Development (OECD)[b] classifies the following as additional risks that exist or are perceived to exist by private investors that are particularly applicable to developing countries:

- Political stability, breach of contract, quality of regulation, and the incidence of regulatory disputes are among the most important political risk concerns for investors. Such political and institutional factors are

(continued on next page)

---

[24] For a review, see Organisation for Economic Co-operation and Development (OECD). 2015. Infrastructure Financing Instruments and Incentives.

[25] PPI Database Global Report. 2020 Annual Report.

[26] PPI Database Global Report. 2021 Half Year (H1) Report.

Box 1 *(continued)*

also those measured by the World Bank through the worldwide governance indicators, which shows that developing regions lag behind in terms of governance quality.[c] Key elements for private investors include the availability of a strong regulatory environment, transparent and competitive procurement processes, and effective contract enforcement arrangements, as well as experience with the use of public–private partnerships, and a track record of successful implementation of such transactions.

• Among the macroeconomic risks, the creditworthiness of a government is the most important counterparty or sovereign risk in developing countries. Inflation is also a chief concern, which includes not just high inflation but the overall volatility of inflation and the central bank's ability to control it. Exchange rate fluctuations increase the currency risk, especially when a project's cash flows are in local currency.

• Market or business risks include risks arising from the business cycle, credit cycle, and the overall health of the financial system. The transparency and availability of information in order to forecast revenue (and costs), and to effectively manage operations, is a key concern in developing markets, incorrectly pricing the business risks of an infrastructure investment. The extent of market or business risk also depends upon the depth and breadth of capital markets, the strength of the domestic banking system, and the ability for banks to act as intermediaries.

With particular reference to Asia and the Pacific, while investors are optimistic about the region's prospects, the majority of them also see numerous challenges which hinder investment.[d] Principal among these are political risk, inadequate regulatory regimes, and concerns around the bankability and commercial viability of large-scale public projects (Figure).

Figure: Perceived Risks to Investing in Infrastructure in Emerging Asian Economies
(excluding the PRC and India)

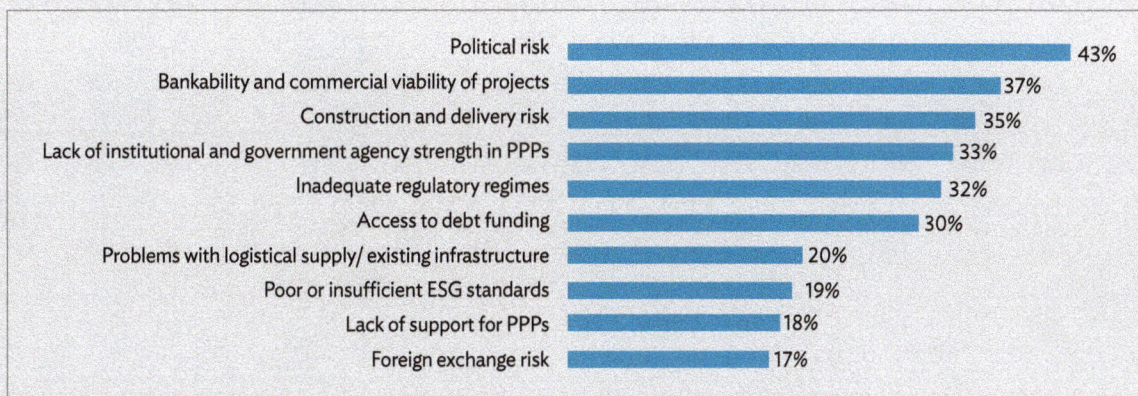

Risk	%
Political risk	43%
Bankability and commercial viability of projects	37%
Construction and delivery risk	35%
Lack of institutional and government agency strength in PPPs	33%
Inadequate regulatory regimes	32%
Access to debt funding	30%
Problems with logistical supply/ existing infrastructure	20%
Poor or insufficient ESG standards	19%
Lack of support for PPPs	18%
Foreign exchange risk	17%

ESG = environmental, social, and governance; PPP = public–private partnership; PRC = People's Republic of China.
Note: Emerging Asian economies include Cambodia, Indonesia, Malaysia, the Philippines, and Thailand.
[a] Probitas Partners. 2020. Infrastructure Institutional Investor Trends: 2019 Survey Results.
[b] OECD. 2015. Risk and Return characteristics of infrastructure investment in low income countries.
[c] World Bank. Worldwide Governance Indicators.
[d] White & Case LLP. 2021. Eye on the future: The outlook for Asian infrastructure. 8 March.
Source: White & Case.

4.1   The Market for Infrastructure Debt

Project Finance Loans

The most widespread financial technique that allows the participation of private capital to unlisted infrastructure is project financing, especially through public–private partnership (PPP) and based on a combination of multiple tranches of loans and equity.[27] Project finance debt has been provided to infrastructure projects mainly in the form of syndicated bank loans, with a pool of banks headed by one or more mandated lead arrangers (MLAs) organizing the financing package for a single borrower.[28]

In 2020, global project finance loans totaled $277.6 billion from 901 deals, representing an 11% drop compared to 2019 (Figure 5). In Q4, volumes reached $93.3 billion, up by 70% from Q3. At the end of the first 9 months of 2021, project finance loans totaled $208 billion from 578 deals, an 11% increase compared to the figures of the previous year. On the other hand, with a total of $4.8 trillion and an increase of 22% compared to 2019, the global bond markets raced in 2020 as major corporate issuers, buoyed by central bank liquidity support, accessed low-cost funds. However, the bond expansion did not include project bonds with issuances amounting to $50.2 billion and registering a decrease of 12% compared to 2019. However, Q3 2021 showed a rebound in project bond issuance that reached $55 billion, an increase of 65% compared to the first 9 months of 2020.

Figure 5: Global Project Finance Loans and Number of Deals, 2017–Q3 2021
($ million)

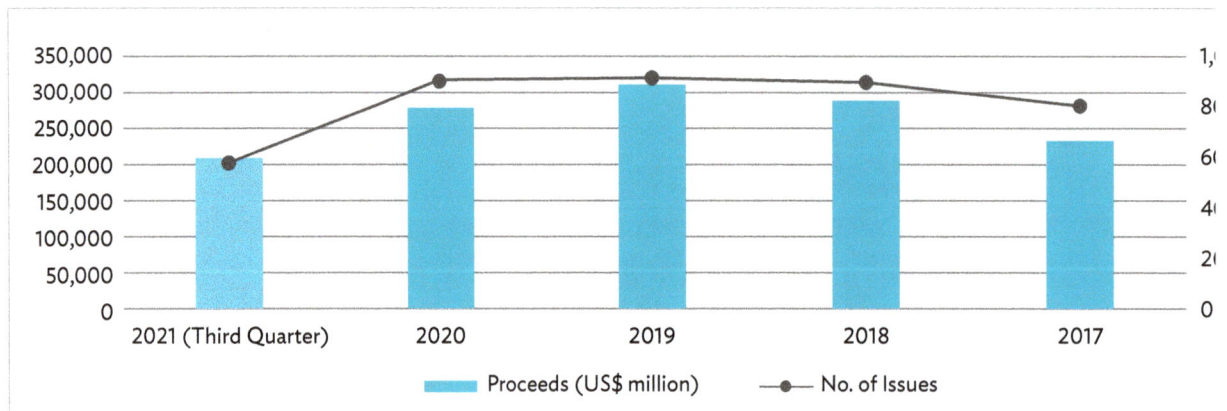

Source: Refinitiv Deal Intelligence.

Despite the drop in absolute terms, project finance loans accounted for a larger share of the global syndicated loans market in 2020, reaching a peak of 7.94% (Figure 6). In the economic turmoil, infrastructure lending demonstrated relative resilience. In fact, in 2020, global syndicated lending totaled $3.5 trillion, registering a 24% drop compared to 2019 and representing the weakest year for lending since 2012.

---

[27]   S. Gatt. 2018. *Project finance in theory and practice: designing, structuring, and financing private and public projects.* Third Edition. Academic Press.
[28]   E.R. Yescombe. 2013. *Principles of project finance.* Academic Press.

Figure 6: Trends in Syndicated and Project Finance Loans, 2017–Q3 2021
($ million)

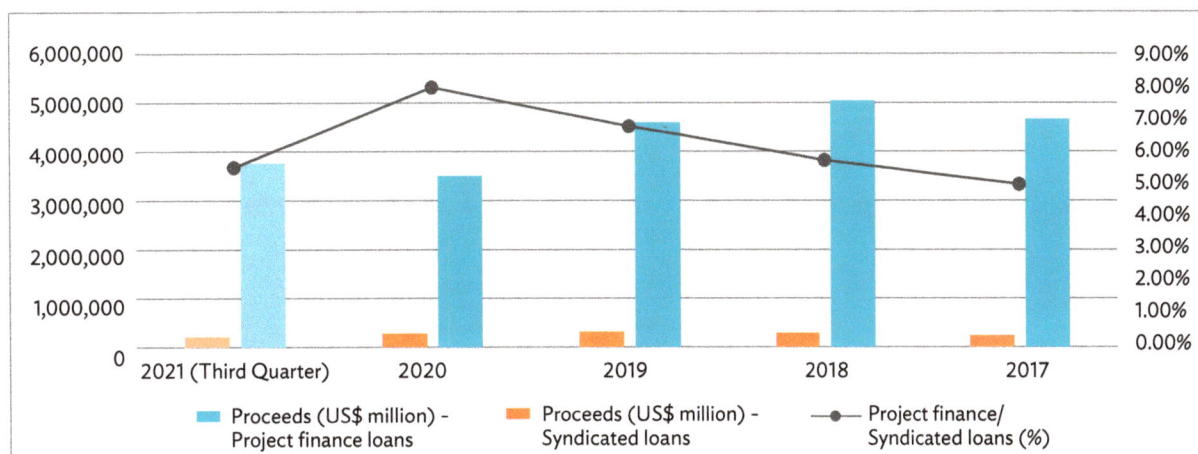

US = United States.
Source: Refinitiv Deal Intelligence

In terms of sector breakdown, power remained the most active sector, accounting for 47.8% of the market activity with total deals amounting to $132.7 billion of the global loan volumes in 2020 (Figure 7). Within the power sector, renewables accounted for 72.4% of the volume at a value of $96.1 billion from 525 deals, in line with the expectations on energy transition for decarbonization. The relevance of renewables was confirmed in the first 9 months of 2021, accounting for 76.3% ($61.4 billion) of the industry. Telecommunications doubled the volume of loans, totaling $13 billion from 32 deals, indicating that the pandemic did not affect the sector. On the contrary, transportation, leisure, and property saw a slash in volumes and value of activities, especially considering recent years' positive trend.

Figure 7: Global Project Finance Market: Breakdown by Sector, 2017–Q3 2021
($ million)

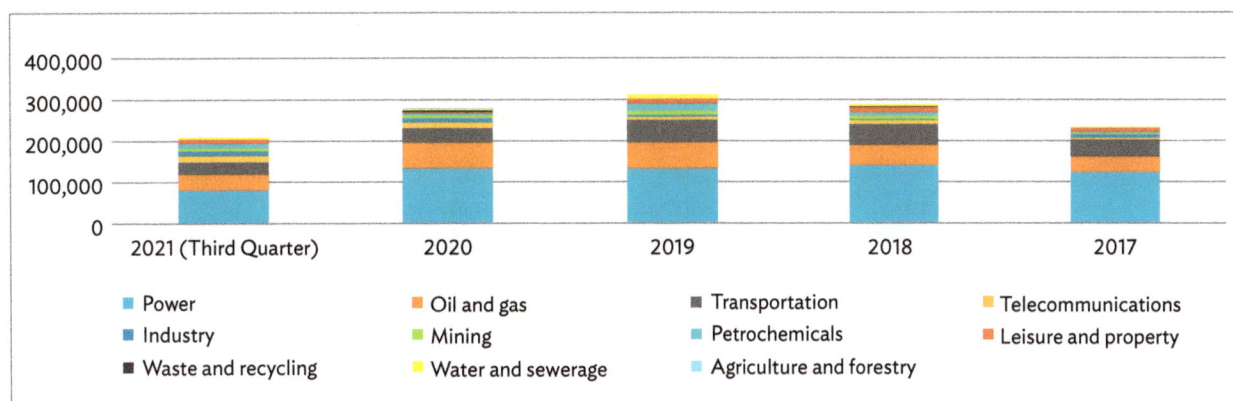

Source: Refinitiv Deal Intelligence.

A look at the geographic breakdown (Figure 8) illustrates a concentration of project finance loans in North America and Western Europe. Compared to 2019, in 2020 North America experienced a growth of 20% in volume of loans, totaling $67.4 billion, while Western Europe had a decline of 1% with $75.3 billion of proceeds. South America, Eastern Europe, Southeast Asia, and South Asia registered a sharp decline, with total aggregated volume in the three regions that passed from $99.4 billion to $43.3 billion in 2020, on average a 57% loss.

Figure 8: Global Project Finance Market: Breakdown by Macro Regions, 2017–Q3 2021
($ million)

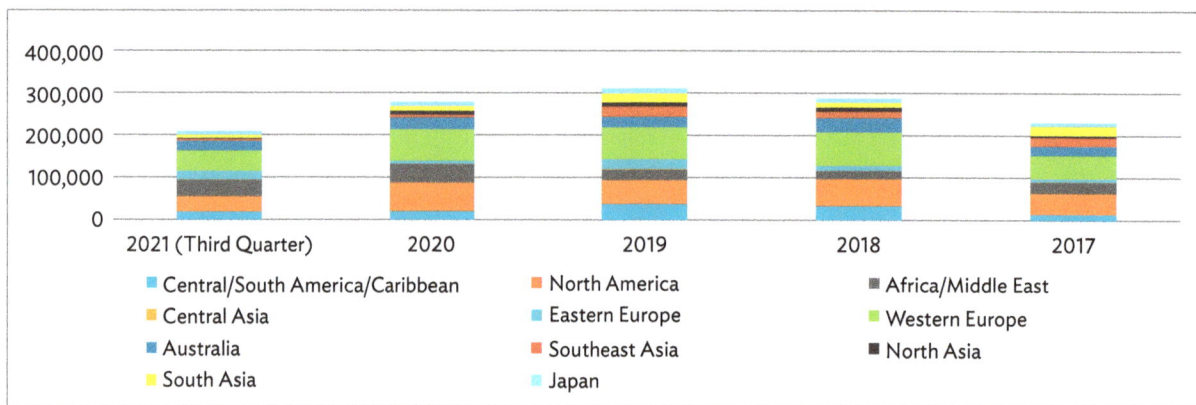

Q3 = third quarter.
Source: Refinitiv Deal Intelligence

With specific reference to Asia and Pacific and Japan, the region saw a significant year-on-year decline of 23.88% over 2019–2020, registering $63.63 billion in project finance loan transactions in 2020, compared with $83.59 billion in 2019.[29] However, the first 9 months of 2021 exhibited a slight increase of 1% from the comparable period in 2020, registering $44.3 billion in project finance loans from 133 issues. Australia led Asia and Pacific and Japan deals, registering 42.3% of total value in 2020, with 53 deals worth $26.9 billion ($21.8 billion in Q3 2021, 49% of the total project finance loans of the region). This is a much higher share of the region's total deal value than the 28.2% of 2019, a year when Australia saw 70 financial closes. India follows with a similar share of regional deals by value at 16.3% in 2020, or $10.4 billion in total value. Japan comes third again, at 33 deals worth $8 billion in 2020.

Figure 10 shows that the power sector, including renewables, remained by far the largest sector in 2020 in Asia and Pacific and Japan, accounting for 46.3% of total deal volume. In 2020, 121 power deals worth $29.5 billion were closed, with 81.3% coming from renewables ($23.9 billion). The comparative figures for 2019 were 99 deals worth $33.8 billion. Oil and gas was the second-largest sector for deal-making in Asia and the Pacific in 2020, at $13.3 billion from 17 deals. Transportation saw regional market shares drop to 19.1% from 27.2% in 2019.

---

[29]   However, despite the pandemic, the number of transactions increased from 191 deals in 2020 up from 173 concluded in 2019.

Figure 9: Asia and Pacific and Japan Project Finance Market: Breakdown by Sector, 2017–Q3 2021
($ million)

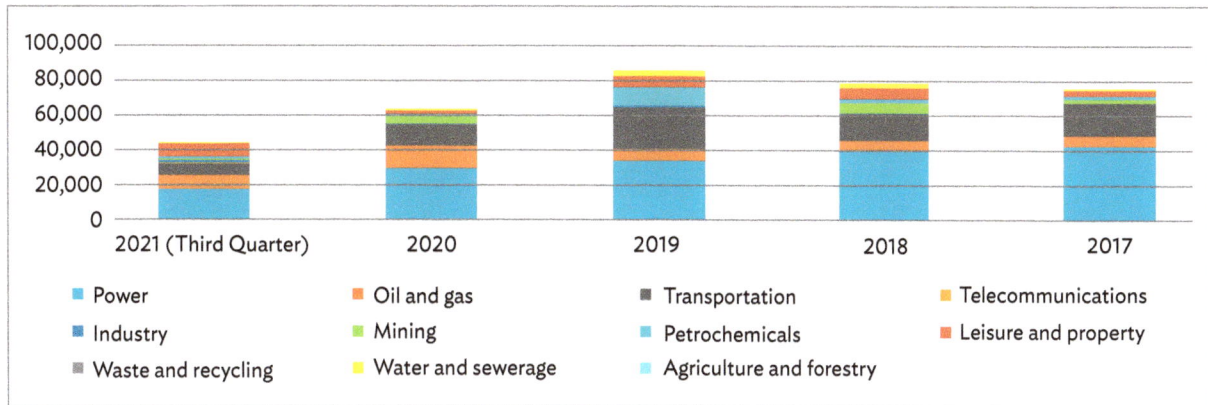

Q3 = third quarter.
Source: Refinitiv Deal Intelligence.

Project Bonds

The alternative to syndicated project finance loans is represented by the financing of infrastructure projects on the bond market via project bonds. Project bonds are issued by special purpose vehicles (SPVs) and sold to either banks or, more frequently, to other bond investors. Compared to project finance loans, project bonds are more standardized capital market instruments, with a higher degree of liquidity and a lower fixed rate cost if the issue size is sufficiently large to generate enough liquidity in the secondary markets, and a longer maturity than the tenors of syndicated loans that banks normally accept. Project bonds also have a number of drawbacks compared with project finance loans, such as, among other things, their costs and complexity, which make them suitable only to transactions of a significant size (e.g., with a bond financing in excess of $100 million), and the proceeds that are drawn all at once upon issuance, which typically results in a negative carry.[30] Negative carry creates severe problems to greenfield infrastructure investments, where engineering, procurement, and construction cost are paid based on milestones and not as a whole lump sum. For these reasons, project bonds are still a limited portion of the total debt committed to infrastructure financing, representing 18.09% of the total infrastructure debt at the end of 2020, with an increase of up to 26.00% in the first 9 months of 2021 (Figure 10).

---

30   For a review of the benefits and drawbacks of financing infrastructure with project bonds, see European PPP Expertise Centre. 2012. *Financing PPPs with project bonds. Issues for Public Procuring Authorities.* Luxembourg: EPEC.

Figure 10: Trends in Project Bonds and Project Finance Loans, 2017–Q3 2021
($ million)

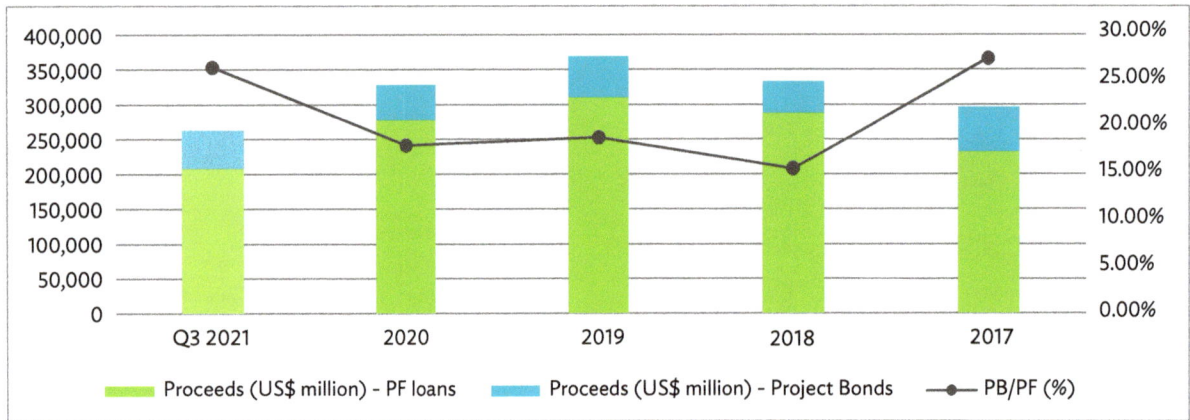

PB = project bonds, PF = project finance, Q3 = third quarter, US = United States.
Source: Refinitiv Deal Intelligence.

The global project bond market is dominated by North America and Europe, Middle East, and Africa (or collectively referred to as EMEA). Asia and Pacific and Japan project bond volume accounts for a minor share (9%) and the market registered a decline of proceeds of nearly 40% in 2020 compared to 2019 (Figure 11). However, Q3 2021 presents a promising trend, totaling $7.8 billion. In comparison, Australia, Indonesia, India, Kazakhstan, and Malaysia issued project bonds in 2020 for $4.7 billion.

Figure 11: Global and Asia and Pacific and Japan Project Bond Market, 2017–Q3 2021
($ million)

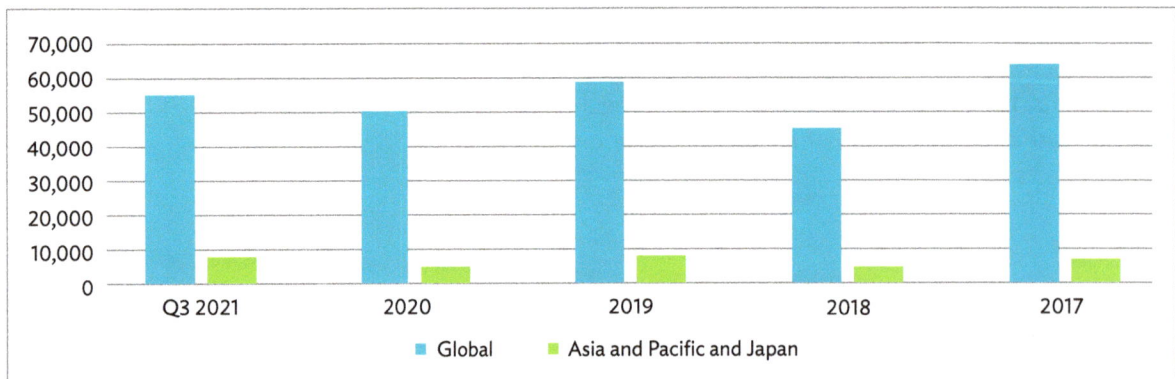

Source: Refinitiv Deal Intelligence.

On the equity side, before mid-2000s almost all infrastructure projects received equity from industrial sponsors and developers; typically the off-taker is the engineering, procurement, and construction contractor; the suppliers; and/or the companies responsible for the operation and maintenance of the asset.

With the recognition of infrastructure as an asset class, there has been a clear increase in global infrastructure private equity fundraising, from $4.8 billion in 2004 to a record peak of almost $100 billion in 2019,[31] representing 37% of total project finance loans in the same year (Figure 12). While fundraising over the year 2020 fell by 15% compared to 2019, this may be a consequence of the challenges of fundraising during lockdown. The time needed to come to fund closing lengthened to 19 months or longer, more for lockdown-related issues rather than to the reluctance of investors to allocate to the asset class. Infrastructure, with their characteristics as an alternative asset class and as an inflation hedge, have proved to be durable attractions for investors. According to Preqin, 2021 will see a bounce-back in equity fundraising for infrastructure, as investors' stated intentions for allocations are very positive over the next 12 months and into the longer term.[32]

Figure 12: Unlisted Infrastructure Equity Fundraising, 2001–2020
($ billion)

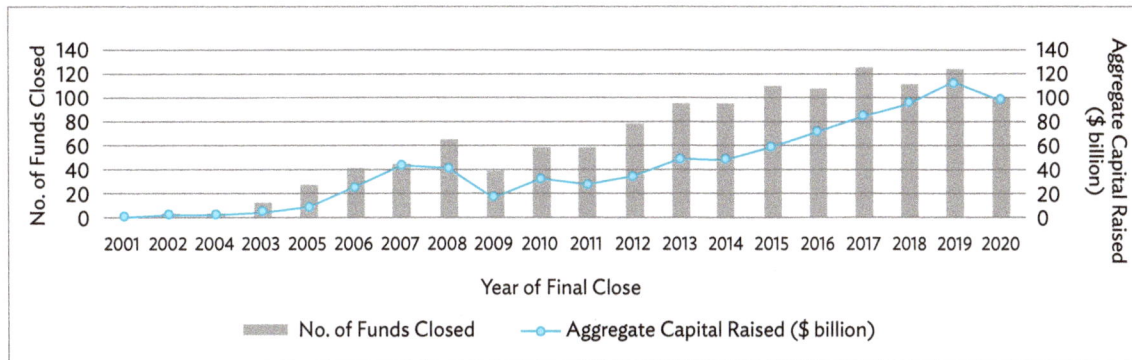

Source: Preqin.

In terms of geographies, 85% of total capital raised in 2020 focused on developed markets (Western Europe and North America); however, Asia experienced a higher compound annual growth rate, i.e., 20% over the period 2005–2020, and it is expected to grow further in the medium term (Figure 13). Private equity funds were indeed expected to be more active in the Asia and Pacific region in 2021,[33] with many being relatively inactive in 2020.[34]

---

[31] Preqin. Global Infrastructure Report (2021).
[32] Adapted from Gatti (2018).
[33] R. Berger. 2017. Implication of Ongoing "Basel IV" Debates: Significant New Constraints to Come for Banks, with Expected Ramifications for European Economy Financing.
[34] For example, the New York-based firm KKR closed its first fund focused on infrastructure investment across Asia and Pacific in January 2021. The $3.9 billion fund, which is a record size for the region, is expected to invest in waste, renewables, power and utilities, telecommunications, and transport infrastructure.

Figure 13: Aggregate Capital Raised by Unlisted Infrastructure Equity Funds by Primary Geographic Focus, 2001–2020

($ billion)

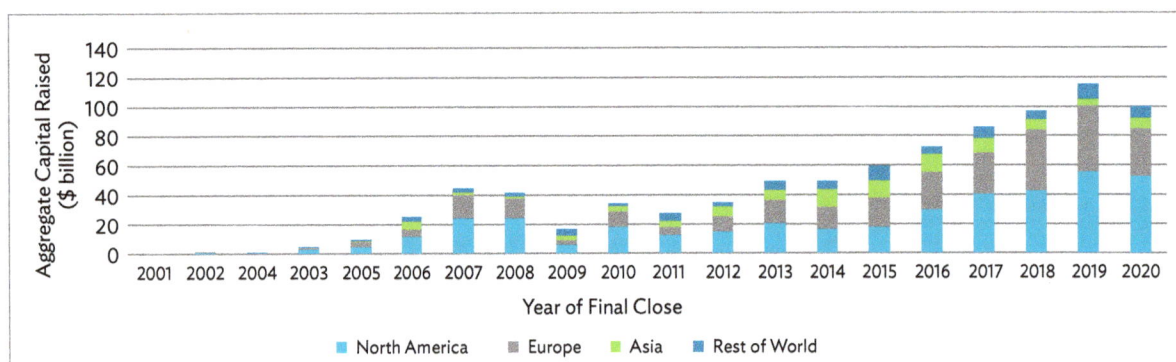

Source: Preqin.

Table 1: Ten Largest Fund Managers by Total Capital Raised for Infrastructure Funds, 2011–2021

Firm	Headquarters	Total Capital Raised in Past 10 Years ($ billion)	Estimated Dry Powder ($ billion)
Global Infrastructure Partners	New York, United States	51.5	19.7
Brookfield Asset Management	Toronto, Canada	48.2	14.0
Macquarie	London, United Kingdom	46.2	12.6
BlackRock	New York, United States	28.7	7.2
Stonepeak Infrastructure Partners	New York, United States	20.7	10.7
EQT	Stockholm, Sweden	17.0	3.2
KB Asset Management	Seoul, Republic of Korea	14.7	4.3
AMP Capital Investors	Sydney, Australia	14.6	3.1
KKR	New York, United States	14.5	5.7
Copenhagen Infrastructure Partners	Copenhagen, Denmark	14.4	6.6

Source: Preqin.

According to Preqin (Table 1), while the number of funds in market continues to grow— from 58 in 2015 to 558 in 2020—the share of capital targeted by the largest fund managers has increased further over the past 12 months. This is due to the fact that the pandemic has pushed investors toward more experienced managers.

Similar to private equity funds, infrastructure funds may pursue different investment strategies with their underlying risk-and-return profiles (Table 2). So far, the large funds are predominantly positioned as generalists pursuing a broad bandwidth of assets. Some funds, however, have a narrower focus, such as on a certain investment stage (greenfield and/or brownfield); geographic

Table 2: Ten Largest Fund Managers by Total Capital Raised for Infrastructure Funds, 2011–2021

Fund	Manager	Manager Country	Vintage	Final Size ($ million)	Fund Structure	Primary Strategy	Primary Sector	Main Geographic Focus	Project Stage Preferences
Global Infrastructure Partners IV	Global Infrastructure Partners	US	2019	22.000	Limited Partnership	Value Added	Diversified	US	Brownfield, Secondary Stage
Brookfield Infrastructure Fund IV	Brookfield Asset Management	Canada	2019	20.000	Limited Partnership	Core	Diversified	US	Brownfield, Greenfield
Global Infrastructure Partners III	Global Infrastructure Partners	US	2016	15.800	Limited Partnership	Value Added	Diversified	US	Brownfield
Brookfield Infrastructure Fund III	Brookfield Asset Management	Canada	2016	14.000	Limited Partnership	Core Plus	Diversified	US	Brownfield, Greenfield
EQT Infrastructure IV	EQT	Sweden	2018	10.195	Limited Partnership	Value Added	Utilities	Europe	Brownfield, Greenfield, Secondary Stage
Copenhagen Infrastructure Partners IV	Copenhagen Infrastructure Partners	Denmark	2020	8.423	SCSp	Core	Renewable Energy	Europe	Greenfield
Global Infrastructure Partners II	Global Infrastructure Partners	US	2012	8.250	Limited Partnership	Value Added	Diversified	US	Brownfield
Antin Infrastructure Partners IV	Antin Infrastructure Partners	France	2019	7.682	SCSp	Value Added	Diversified	Europe	Brownfield
KKR Global Infrastructure Investors III	KKR	US	2018	7.400	Limited Partnership	Core Plus	Diversified	US	Brownfield, Secondary Stage
Stonepeak Infrastructure Partners III	Stonepeak Infrastructure Partners	US	2018	7.303	Limited Partnership	Value Added	Diversified	US	Brownfield, Greenfield

US = United States.
Source: Preqin.

location (individual country, Europe, the United States, OECD, emerging markets); and/or sector (e.g., individual sectors, a selection of sectors, or all sectors) accompanied by different sizes, terms, and structures.

In terms of investors, the infrastructure investor pool consisted of almost 4,000 institutions as of the beginning of 2020. This represents 35% of the total investor base, and represents an increase of around 50% compared to end of 2015.[35] Despite the increase in the number of investors targeting infrastructure, their actual allocation to unlisted infrastructure equity as a percentage

---

[35]   Preqin. Global Infrastructure Report (2021).

of their total assets is still very small.[36] Most of these investors have relatively high liquidity needs, and the illiquidity of infrastructure investments means they cannot commit too much to the asset class. Table 3 provides the 10 largest equity investors in infrastructure by total capital allocated to infrastructure at the beginning of 2021.

Table 3: Ten Largest Equity Investors in Infrastructure—Global, Q1 2021

Investor	Investor Type	Location	Allocation to Infrastructure ($ billion)	Assets under Management ($ billion)	Infrastructure as a % of Total Asset under Management
National Wealth Fund	Sovereign Wealth Fund	Russian Federation	53.7	134	40.0%
CPP Investment Board	Public Pension Fund	Canada	28.7	420	6.8%
DWS Group	Asset Manager	Germany	27.6	838	3.3%
MetLife Insurance Company	Insurance Company	United States	24.5	506	4.8%
National Pension Service	Public Pension Fund	Republic of Korea	23.6	673	3.5%
CDPQ	Public Pension Fund	Canada	21.9	245	8.9%
AMP Capital Investors	Asset Manager	Australia	20.1	135	14.9%
OMERS	Public Pension Fund	Canada	19.9	91	21.8%
NORD/LB	Bank	Germany	19.2	150	12.8%
Rabobank Group	Bank	Netherlands	19.4	697	2.8%

Q1 = first quarter.
Source: Preqin.

---

[36]   OECD. 2021. Annual Survey of Large Pension Funds and Public Pension Reserve Funds.

KEY TRENDS AND COOPERATION MODELS BETWEEN BANKS AND INSTITUTIONAL INVESTORS

5

As discussed in the previous section, banks are the key actors in the market for infrastructure lending, given their skills and competencies in originating and structuring project finance transactions. While banks traditionally have been responsible for almost 90% of project finance loans (footnote 29), the relative share of bank finance to total infrastructure finance has decreased in recent years and a new pool of liquidity has grown outside the banking sector.[37] These new investors belong to the category of long-term institutional investors, which consider infrastructure an appealing asset class given its features and its fit with asset and liability management policies. In this context, Box 4 shows the growing importance of infrastructure within investors' portfolio.

Unlocking the huge liquidity available among institutional investors with pension funds and life insurers in OECD countries holding $35 trillion[38] and $15.3 trillion,[39] respectively, in assets in 2020, would substantially help finance the infrastructure gap. This is particularly important given the relative retreat of bank lenders from many markets.

Over the last decade, nonbank infrastructure debt has grown in importance as project financing from banks has come under pressure following the global financial crisis (GFC). After the crisis, the international regulatory response was implemented mostly through the Basel III accords and gradually phased-in between 2013 and the end of 2018. The Basel III regime has drastically increased capital and liquidity requirements for banks, making capital-intensive and illiquid assets far less attractive. Basel III requires increased provision of liquidity, both in the short and long run. Adopting a two-pronged approach, the newly introduced liquidity coverage ratio requires banks to have sufficient high-quality liquid assets in order to meet anticipated (net) outflows under a 30-day stress scenario, while the net stable funding ratio requires banks to match long-term assets with long-term liabilities and thus rely less on the cheaper but more volatile inter-banking market in order to avoid a maturity mismatch.[40]

The impact of Basel III on infrastructure finance has been twofold: an increase in bank funding costs, which is reflected in an increase in loan spreads for infrastructure projects; and a decrease in infrastructure debt maturity, creating a growing mismatch between the amount and time horizon of available capital and that of infrastructure projects.

[37] Financial Stability Board. 2018. *Evaluation of the effects of financial regulatory reforms on infrastructure finance*. 20 November.
[38] OECD. 2021. Pension Funds in Figures.
[39] OECD. 2021. Insurance Statistics 2020.
[40] Yescombe (2013), p. 484 and T. Ma. 2016. Basel III and the Future of Project Finance Funding. *Michigan Business and Entrepreneurial Law Review*. 6 (1). pp. 109–126.

Box 4: Infrastructure as an Asset Class

The characteristics of infrastructure assets have sustained the growth of assets under management (AUMs), enabling the recognition of infrastructure as an alternative asset class. The AUMs of the global unlisted infrastructure market stood at $655 billion, which represented 8.5% of the total private capital under management as of June 2020. Of the $655 billion, the capital committed in funds that had been called up by fund managers (unrealized value) was $420 billion, while capital raised that had not been invested (dry powder) was $235 billion. Despite the opportunity cost of the dry powder, the increasing investor appetite for unlisted infrastructure helped to drive the proportion of the uncommitted capital to approximately 35% (Figure).

Figure: Private Capital Assets under Management by Asset Class (2010–2020) and Unlisted Infrastructure Assets under Management (2000–2020)

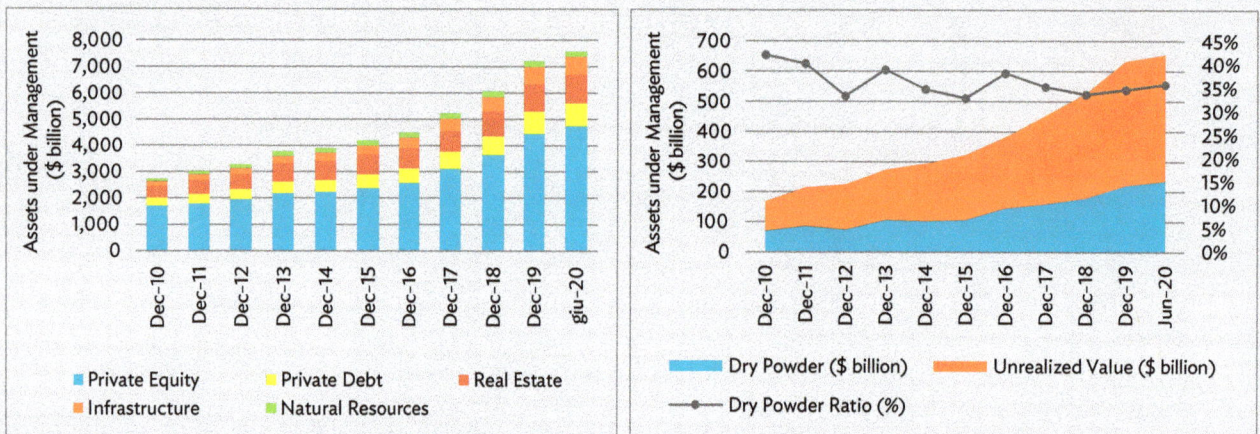

Source: Preqin Pro.

In terms of investment strategies, the heterogeneous nature of infrastructure has provided investors with an extensive range of risk-and-return profiles within the asset class referring to the selection of the infrastructure projects to invest in. The allocation of the AUM suggests that investors are recognizing the potential of diversification in equity investments with reference to the different risk-and-return profiles offered by infrastructure assets (Figure).[a] Likewise, private debt has become a growing component of the unlisted infrastructure financing with an increase of 350% since 2014 to $86 billion by the end of June 2020.

Box 4 (continued)

Figure: Unlisted Infrastructure Assets under Management by Primary Strategy, 2010–2020

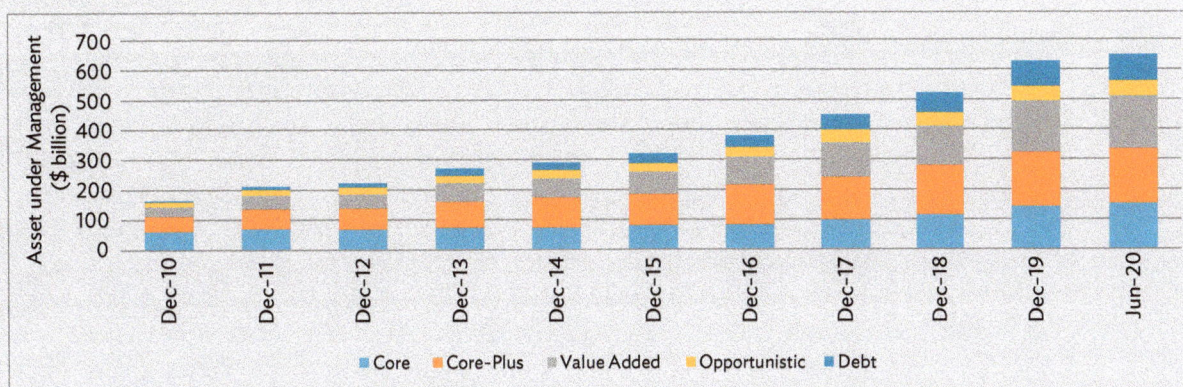

Core   Core-Plus   Value Added   Opportunistic   Debt

[a] There are five key strategies for infrastructure investment with varying levels of risk-and-return profiles of infrastructure assets. Core, Core-Plus, Value Added, and Opportunistic represent equity investments. See https://www.preqin.com for a complete description of the investment strategies.

Source: Preqin Pro.

While Ma (2016) estimated an increase of 60–110 basis points in funding costs for banks compared to the Basel II regime,[41] Walter (2016) registered an increase of margins from roughly 50–100 basis points pre-crisis to 250–350 basis points post-crisis.[42] The Financial Stability Board recorded an appreciable spike in loan spreads during the GFC, which registered a decline post-crisis, but have not returned to pre-crisis levels. [43] This surge in spreads has increased competition as institutional investors, which have inherently higher return requirements, can compete with banks on pricing. According to Blanc-Brude et al. (2017),[44] the duration of unlisted infrastructure debt also decreased significantly since the turn of the century and in the wake of the GFC, and is now on a par with general corporate debt. In this context, Hallak and Wambeke (2014) reported a substantial decline in the average maturity of European PPP loans, from over 20 years pre-crisis to around 10 years post-crisis.[45] These findings are echoed by the Financial Stability Board, which reported an overall decrease in maturity by around 3 years for infrastructure loans. Finally, Wouter and De Moor (2019) documented that over 2013–2016, the Basel III regime resulted in a reduction in the average length of the loan tenor by about 2.3 years.[46]

---

[41] T. Ma. 2016. Basel III and the Future of Project Finance Funding. *Michigan Business and Entrepreneurial Law Review*. 6 (1). pp. 109–126.

[42] I. Walter. 2016. *The Infrastructure Finance Challenge: A Report by the Working Group on Infrastructure Finance, Stern School of Business, New York University*. New York: Open Book Publishers.

[43] Financial Stability Board. 2018. *Evaluation of the effects of financial regulatory reforms on infrastructure finance*. 20 November.

[44] F. Blanc-Brude et al. 2017. *Private Infrastructure Debt Broad Market Indices: Benchmarking Europe's Private Infrastructure Debt Market 2000–2016*. EDHEC Infrastructure Institute-Singapore.

[45] I. Hallak and M. Wambeke. 2014. The New Landscape of the Infrastructure Debt Market: Opportunities for Banks and Institutional Investors: Report for the Centre of Financial Services at Vlerick Business School.

[46] T. Wouter and L. De Moor. 2019. Loan Tenor in Project Finance. *International Journal of Managing Projects in Business*. 12 (3). pp. 825–842.

While under the Basel III regime, risk weights for assets have been left untouched, increase in risk weights in the so-called Basel IV regime will be gradually phased-in by 2022, especially in case of specialized lending including project and infrastructure finance.[47] In response, banks may further downsize long-term and specialized lending activities, and reduce long-term lending, expand (noncore) asset sales as a part of general portfolio management, and focus more on an "originate-to-distribute" business model where assets are no longer held until maturity. In sum, there is a general expectation of another round of deleveraging by banks and a more capital markets-oriented financing for infrastructure assets once Basel IV reaches full implementation and implications of Basel III start to show their effects in full. Further, the COVID-19 pandemic can affect the capital and liquidity buffers of banks. In fact, expiration of COVID-19 support programs to secure credit flow can trigger higher defaults on existing loans and force banks to increase provisions and apply higher risk weights on new non-guaranteed loans. [48] As a result, provisions to loan-loss reserves may have to be raised to absorb the termination of repayment moratoria.

Figure 14: Main Reasons for Investing in Alternatives by Asset Class

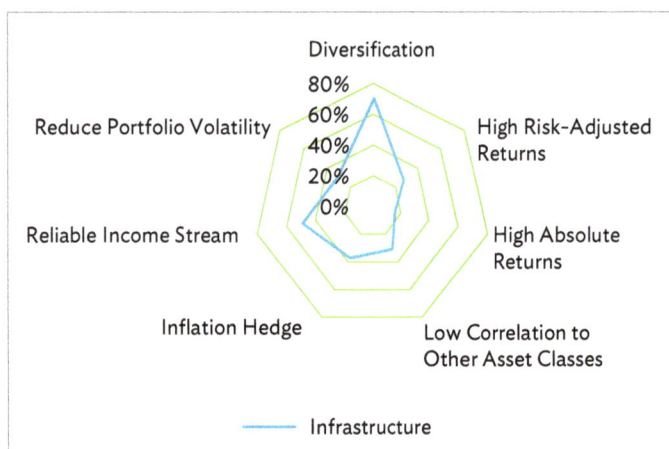

Source: Preqin investor interviews, November 2020.

These circumstances strengthen an opening for institutional investors in infrastructure investments, specifically in debt financing. In fact, it is commonly agreed that these investors with long-term liabilities and low risk appetite seem suited to invest in infrastructure assets with low risk profile.[49] As shown by Figure 14, investors are interested in purchasing infrastructure assets to diversify their portfolios because of the low correlation of infrastructure with traditional asset classes. Moreover, the investment characteristics of infrastructure are associated with predictable (i.e., due to long-term contracts) and stable (i.e., due to low volatility for inelastic demand) cash flows over the long term, and are an inflation hedge. Infrastructure investments thus can provide liability matching for institutional investors, who have become more aligned to investments with long-term income (yield-driven investors) results as opposed to investments with short-term capital gain results (internal rate of return-driven investors). Accordingly, the proportion of investors looking to increase their infrastructure allocations over the next 12 months jumped from 38% in 2019 to 54% in 2020, the highest since 2016.[50]

Moreover, while market analyses suggest that unlisted equity funds are the most common vehicle of institutional infrastructure financing, 18% of investors surveyed by Probitas Partners are currently actively targeting debt.[51] Institutional investors' debt financing has increased mostly through project bond issuance, but also through various co-investment models with banks. Under this new

---

47   S. Gatti. 2020. BASEL IV Impact on specialized lending and project finance. SDA Bocconi School of Management.
48   According to the IMF Global Financial Stability Report (April 2021), guaranteed loans accounted for almost 2% of total loans on average as of Q3 2020, though in some countries that figure was as high as 4%.
49   R. Della Croce and S. Gatti. 2014. *Financing infrastructure: international trends*. Paris: OECD.
50   Preqin. 2021. Investor Outlook Alternative Assets H1 2021.
51   Probitas Partners. 2019. Infrastructure Institutional Investor Trends: 2019 Survey Results.

approach, banks originate a transaction to "resell" or "distribute" to debt capital markets rather than to keep the assets on their loan books until maturity. This cooperation can take different forms:

(i)   the debt fund model;

(ii)   the direct lending model, which can be done either in a partnership or co-investment with a bank, or with a direct origination of infrastructure loans by institutional investors; and

(iii) the securitization model.

In the following sections, the three models are presented and accompanied by examples and case studies, both in Asia and globally. Cases and examples have been collected through multiple methodologies, including desk research, anecdotal evidence,[52] and case study methodology. The small number of cooperation initiatives between banks and nonbank investors implemented worldwide, as well as their dependence on the specific context in which they have been implemented, make the sample selection and analysis through statistical techniques a challenging endeavor. For this reason, we have adopted a qualitative research design and applied purposive case selection[53] to build a sample that is both representative and shows a useful variation on the forms of cooperation presented.

5.1   The Debt Fund Model

Infrastructure debt funds are relatively new players in the field of project finance (see Box 5 to review the most recent trends in unlisted infrastructure debt funds). These funds are investment vehicles that provide debt to infrastructure projects under the form of direct loans and, to a lesser extent, bonds. The debt fund model is probably the easiest way to approach the infrastructure market for institutional investors, even for the less sophisticated ones and those without a specific, dedicated team to invest in relative assets. With this model, investors make an unfunded commitment to the limited partnership, which is drawn during the term of the fund that is raised and managed by investment professionals who screen, analyze, invest, monitor, and implement value creation actions in infrastructure projects. The strategic asset allocation is defined from the outset of the deal, which allows institutional investors to select the fund that best suits their investment needs, for instance achieving a risk diversification advantage. The success of the debt fund model is contingent on a strong deal flow.

While debt funds can represent a vital channel for funneling institutional investors' money to infrastructure, the drawback is that—compared to the other models, i.e., direct lending or securitizations—such funds are based on fixed and pre-agreed investment criteria. Moreover, the shorter-term focus of unlisted infrastructure funds, which typically have a private equity structure and a 10-year maturity, is not fully consistent with the long-term hold philosophy of core infrastructure but seems more suited to turnaround deals.[54] This delegated form of investing, in

---

52   Between June and September 2021, we conducted five interviews with prominent infrastructure experts who asked to remain anonymous.
53   Purposive sampling is widely used in qualitative research for the identification and selection of information-rich cases related to the phenomenon of interest, see J. W. Creswell and C. N. Poth. 2016. *Qualitative Inquiry and Research Design*. Sage publications; J. Seawright and J. Gerring. 2008. Case Selection Techniques in Case Study Research: A Menu of Qualitative and Quantitative Options. *Political Research Quarterly*. 61(2). pp. 294–308.
54   A. Monk and R. Sharma. 2015. Re-Intermediating Investment Management: A Relational Contracting Approach. *Stanford Global Projects Center Working Paper*.

addition, has come under scrutiny in recent years as it showed some limits in terms of misaligned interests, high fees, poor returns, and short-termism embedded in certain third-party management agreements.[55] For instance, management fees of infrastructure funds appear oriented toward private equity-style schemes, although in the past 10 vintage years it has remained below the industry standard of 2%, except for 2013 (Figure 15). This trend could be explained by the growing weight of Core-Plus and Value Added strategies of infrastructure funds (Box 5, figure on p. 38) that are more similar to private equity investments. However, while the private equity fee model may be suited to higher risk/return strategies, most infrastructure investors are looking for fees to reflect the types of assets being invested in and the levels of returns expected when gaining exposure to lower risk/ return infrastructure assets.

Figure 15: Average Management Fee during Investment Period by Fund Type

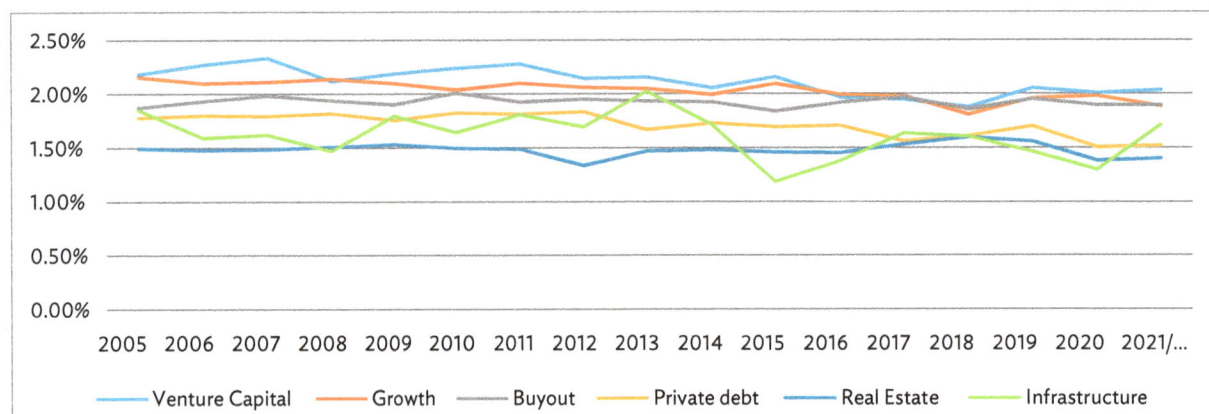

Source: Preqin Private Capital Fund Terms Advisor 2020.

The classic principal–agent problem, thus, is a key concern associated to indirect delegated investing: the intermediary may engage in behaviors that benefit portfolio managers rather than the investors, growing fees at the expense of returns, investing at market peaks when expected returns are modest, and exit transactions prematurely to facilitate fundraising.[56] For example, during 1990s, carry interests[57] had the unforeseen issue of undermining the rationale of institutional investors for infrastructure investing through funds.[58] If in the beginning, fund managers drove the infrastructure investment model (e.g., Macquarie), the engagement of long-term investors to work through

---

55   J. S. Bachher and A. Monk. 2013. Platforms and Vehicles for Institutional Co- Investing. *Rotman International Journal of Pension Management.* 6 (1); L. Fang, I. Victoria, and J. Lerner. 2015. The Disintermediation of Financial Markets: Direct Investing in Private Equity. *Journal of Financial Economics.* 116 (1). Elsevier: 160–78.

56   For a review of these agency problems, see for example: S. Kaplan and A. Schoar. 2005. Private Equity Performance: Returns, Persistence, and Capital Flows. *The Journal of Finance 60* (4). Wiley Online Library: 1,791–1,823; U. Axelson et al. 2013. Borrow Cheap, Buy High? The Determinants of Leverage and Pricing in Buyouts. *The Journal of Finance.* 68 (6). Wiley Online Library: 2223–67.

57   Carry structures typically have the effect of creating an option on the fund performance for the benefit of the manager (the general partner). Because the value of the option increases as the volatility of the underlying asset grows, managers can increase the value of their portfolio of carried interest by rising the volatility of their investments.

58   G. Clark et al. 2012. The New Era of Infrastructure Investing. *Pensions: An International Journal.* 17 (2). pp. 103–111.

Box 5: Infrastructure Debt Funds at Global Level

The number of infrastructure debt funds that have held final close indicates the growing interests of the asset class for investors, amounting to 170 in the 10-year period from 2010 to 2020 (Figure).

Figure: Unlisted Infrastructure Funds Closed by Primary Strategy, 2001–2020

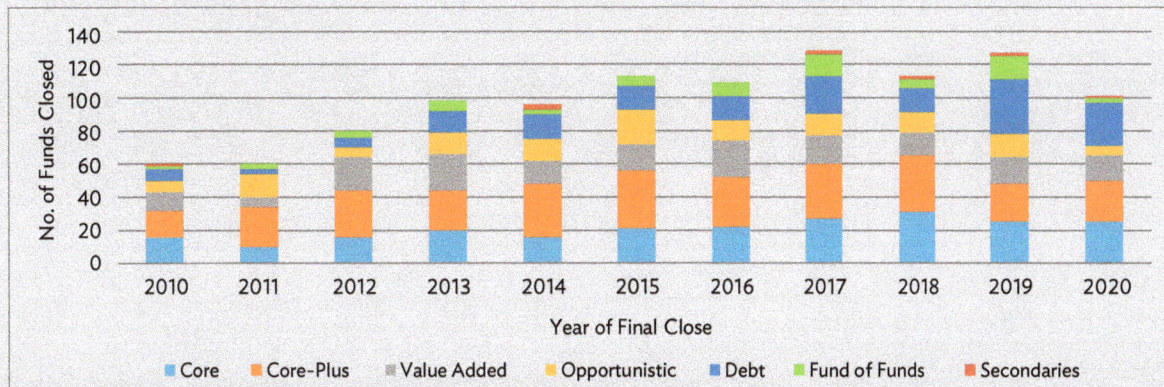

Source: Preqin Pro.

For the same period, fund managers have roughly raised $88 billion for infrastructure debt strategy representing almost 12% of the total capital committed by investors. Although the amount is limited compared to alternative private investment categories, it is substantial relative to the volume raised in 2010 that was approximately $1 billion, remarking the appeal of the asset class (Figure).

Figure: Aggregate Capital Raised by Unlisted Infrastructure Funds by Primary Strategy, 2001–2020

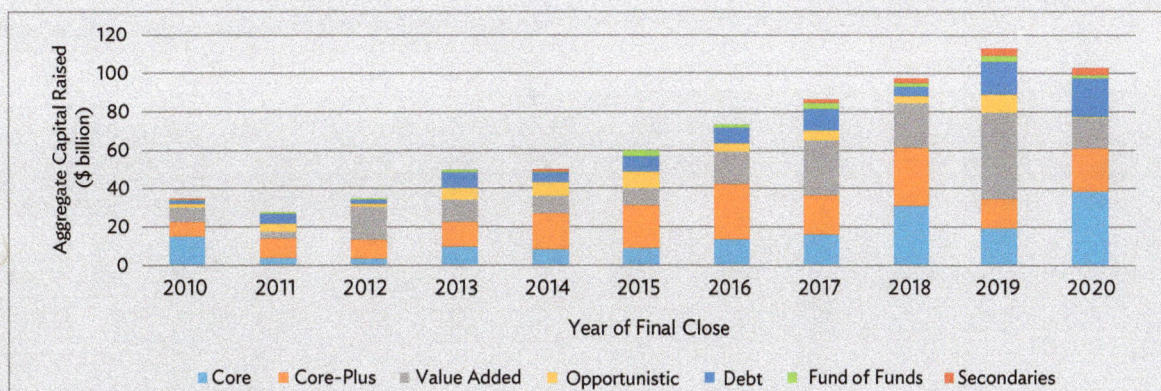

Source: Preqin Pro.

Infrastructure debt managers differ in their exposure to development risk of infrastructure projects. Generally, debt strategies focus on established, brownfield investments that provide essential public services and benefit from stable and predictable cash flows. Additionally, investments can include attractive greenfield assets where construction risk is mitigated and where revenue projections are based on contracted and/or regulated cash flows (Table). Infrastructure investments benefit from financial covenants and/or collateral that can help lenders with downside protections at attractive yields relative to similar public corporate peers. Lender protections, coupled with stable cash flow potential due to the essential services provided by the assets, enable lenders to lend to infrastructure assets for 20, 30, 40, or possibly 50 years. Despite the investment strategy is diversified referring to sectors and stages, the essential targets of largest infrastructure fund managers (Brookfield, BlackRock, Macquarie, etc.) are high-income countries, which is actually logical for vehicles offering a high level of capital protection to their limited partnerships. Nonetheless, the geographies in which the funds operate are distributed across three central regions that are Asia (30%),

Box 5 *(continued)*

Europe (28%), and the United States (22%), although their average size differs ($288 million in Asia, $563 million in Europe, and $763 million in the United States). As for the Asian market, for instance, there are investment companies such as Global Infrastructure Partners and AMP Capital Investors that are running funds primarily committed in the energy, transportation, and utility sectors with a committed capital of $5 billion (target size and raising capital as of October 2021) and $300 million, respectively.

Table: Largest Unlisted Infrastructure Funds with Primary Strategy in Debt Closed between 2010 and 2020

Fund	Manager	Manager Country	Vintage	Final Size ($ billion)	Fund Structure	Primary Strategy	Primary Sector	Main Geographic Focus	Project Stage Preferences
BlackRock Infrastructure Debt	BlackRock	US	2013	7.571		Debt/Mezz.	Diversified	Europe	Brownfield, Greenfield, Secondary Stage
EIG Energy Fund XVI	EIG Global Energy Partners	US	2013	6.000	Limited Partnership	Debt/Mezz., Primary	Energy	US	Brownfield, Secondary Stage
Macquarie Infrastructure Partners IV	Macquarie Infrastructure and Real Assets (MIRA)	UK	2018	5.000	Limited Partnership	Debt/Mezz., Primary	Diversified	US	Brownfield, Greenfield, Secondary Stage
EIG Energy Fund XV	EIG Global Energy Partners	US	2010	4.121	Limited Partnership	Debt/Mezz., Primary	Energy	US	Brownfield, Secondary Stage
AMP Capital Infrastructure Debt Fund IV	AMP Capital Investors	Australia	2019	4.000	Limited Partnership	Debt/Mezz.	Diversified	US	Brownfield
Westbourne Infrastructure Debt Fund Program 1	Westbourne Capital	Australia	2015	3.651		Debt/Mezz.	Diversified	Diversified Multi-Regional	Brownfield, Greenfield
EIG Energy Fund XVII	EIG Global Energy Partners	US	2017	3.100	Limited Partnership	Debt/Mezz., Primary	Energy	US	Brownfield, Secondary Stage
Westbourne Infrastructure Debt Fund Program 3	Westbourne Capital	Australia	2018	3.000		Debt/Mezz.	Diversified	Diversified Multi-Regional	Brownfield, Greenfield
Carlyle Energy Mezzanine Opportunities Fund II	Carlyle Group	US	2016	2.800	Limited Partnership	Debt/Mezz.	Energy	US	Greenfield
Brookfield Infrastructure Debt Fund II	Brookfield Asset Management	Canada	2020	2.700	Limited Partnership	Debt/Mezz.	Diversified	US	Brownfield, Greenfield

continued on next page

Box 5 (*continued*)

Fund	Manager	Manager Country	Vintage	Final Size ($ billion)	Fund Structure	Primary Strategy	Primary Sector	Main Geographic Focus	Project Stage Preferences
AMP Capital Infrastructure Debt Fund III	AMP Capital Investors	Australia	2016	2.500	Limited Partnership	Debt/Mezz.	Diversified	US	Brownfield
CCCC First Phase Equity Investment Fund	CCCC Fund Management	PRC	2015	2.343	LLP	Debt/ Mezz., Primary	Diversified	Asia	Greenfield
Beijing Zhong Jiao Zhao Yin Road Bridge Equity Fund	CCCC Fund Management	PRC	2016	2.246		Debt/ Mezz., Primary	Transport	Asia	Greenfield
KIAMCO Power Energy Private Fund Special Asset Trust 3	KDB Infrastructure Investments Asset Management	Republic of Korea	2013	2.236	Trust	Debt/ Mezz., Primary	Energy	Asia	Greenfield
Blue Ocean Fund	EnTrust Global	US	2017	2.100		Debt/Mezz.	Transport	Europe	Brownfield, Greenfield, Secondary Stage
BlackRock Global Infrastructure Debt Funds	BlackRock	US	2017	1.670	Limited Partnership	Debt/Mezz.	Diversified	US	Brownfield, Greenfield, Secondary Stage
Leading Asia's Private Sector Infrastructure Fund	Asian Development Bank	Philippines	2016	1.500	Trust	Debt/ Mezz., Primary	Diversified	Asia	Brownfield, Greenfield, Secondary Stage
Westbourne Infrastructure Debt Fund Program 2	Westbourne Capital	Australia	2015	1.500		Debt/Mezz.	Diversified	Diversified Multi-Regional	Brownfield, Greenfield
Infranode II	INFRANODE	Sweden	2019	1.476	Limited Liability Company	Debt/ Mezz., Primary	Diversified	Europe	Brownfield, Greenfield, Secondary Stage
Global Infrastructure Partners Capital Solutions Fund II	Global Infrastructure Partners	US	2020	1.400	SCSp	Debt/Mezz.	Energy	US	Brownfield, Greenfield, Secondary Stage

continued on next page

Box 5 (*continued*)

Fund	Manager	Manager Country	Vintage	Final Size ($ billion)	Fund Structure	Primary Strategy	Primary Sector	Main Geographic Focus	Project Stage Preferences
Global Infrastructure Partners Spectrum Fund	Global Infrastructure Partners	US	2019	1.400	Limited Partnership	Debt/Mezz.	Energy	US	Brownfield
European Infra Senior 1	AXA Investment Managers – Real Assets	France	2016	1.396		Debt/Mezz.	Diversified	Europe	Brownfield, Greenfield, Secondary Stage
Carlyle Energy Mezzanine Opportunities Fund	Carlyle Group	US	2011	1.380	Limited Partnership	Debt/Mezz.	Energy	US	Greenfield
Macquarie Infrastructure Debt Fund (UK Inflation Linked) 1	Macquarie Infrastructure Debt Investment Solutions	Australia	2014	1.293	Limited Partnership	Debt/Mezz.	Diversified	Europe	Brownfield, Greenfield, Secondary Stage
MEAG Infrastructure Debt Fund II	MEAG - A Munich Re Company	Germany	2020	1.250	SICAV-RAIF	Debt/Mezz.	Diversified	Europe	Brownfield, Greenfield

PRC = People's Republic of China, UK = United Kingdom, US = United States.
Source: Preqin Pro.

Together with traditional infrastructure specialists, top asset managers in the field of infrastructure debt are affiliated with insurance or reinsurance companies, such as Allianz Global Investors, AXA IM, and MEAG, that have established captive general partners. For example, AXA IM has raised a total amount of $14.43 billion across its infrastructure debt strategies since 2014 targeting digital infrastructure, renewable energy, and rail transportation in Europe, while Allianz Global Investors has reached total capital commitments for $8.16 billion, investing in more than 65 infrastructure debt transactions in 17 countries to date.[a]

With geographies, sectors, and stages, an approach to classify the investment strategies is the credit quality of the infrastructure asset class that debt funds target. Investments are typically safe investment-grade opportunities with contracted or regulated entities that have established performance track records and stable projected trends. These assets provide portfolio diversification through investment in assets that are generally not available in the public markets and may provide an add-on risk premium over corporate bonds. With the eligibility of participating in bank syndications, club deals, or lending directly to infrastructure projects, the strategies can be classified as follows (see next Table):[b]

- **Capital preservation** (i.e., MEAG infrastructure debt fund II). It entails a direct investment in privately traded and mostly not rated senior secured investment-grade debt that returns a gross internal rate of return (IRR) ranging 3%–5%. Senior loans have the lowest level of risk of all financing instruments

Box 5 *(continued)*

being secured by standard collaterals and covenants (i.e., maintaining reserve and liquidity accounts, debt service and/or maintenance reserves). In contrast to bonds, the terms and conditions of senior loans can be customized to the individual requirements of each project or asset. Specifically, the interest and principal payments can be adjusted to match the cash flows of the (project) company. Generally, the limited partnerships are insurance companies and pension funds that are interested in long-term stable and predictable incomes derived from the long-term maturity of the loans (up to 30 years).

- **Enhance returns** (i.e., Brookfield infrastructure debt fund II). It encompasses investment strategies from senior to junior debt with a target gross IRRs ranging 6%–10%. If operating in non-investment-grade debt, investments tend to have shorter maturities and shorter duration, ranging between greenfield and browfield projects. Subordinated debt will be serviced after the senior debt and generally has a greater likelihood of default. Therefore, junior debt requires a higher interest rate in order to reflect this increased level of risk.

- **Opportunistic** (i.e., Carlyle Energy Mezzanine Opportunities Fund). It involves a higher exposure to subordinate debt as mezzanine. Mezzanine financing is a capital resource that sits between (lower risk) senior debt and (higher risk) equity that has debt features and can have (when warranted) equity features as well. Mezzanine capital is a subordinated debt, long-term instrument with a claim on a company's assets which is senior only to that of the common shares. Infrastructure investment funds that target subordinated debt expect to generate a gross IRR higher then 10%, rivaling the return objectives for Core-Plus infrastructure equity funds. An example of the strategy is provided by AMP Capital Infrastructure Debt Fund IV that has financed a greenfield mezzanine facility of $280 million to Mainstream Renewable Power in 2020, complementing the $1.25 billion of senior project finance debt raised from multilateral lenders for the construction of three wind and solar energy projects in Chile.

Table: Common Characteristics of Infrastructure Debt Strategies

	CAPITAL PRESERVATION Seeks to prevent loss of capital through exposure to high-quality credits	RETURN-ENHANCING Seeks to maximize returns with exposure to crossover credits	OPPORTUNISTIC Seeks to generate equity-like returns by financing the lowest quality assets
Debt seniority	Senior debt	Primarily senior debt/ junior debt	Junior debt, possibly with equity features
Credit quality	Investment grade	Primarily investment grade	Non-investment grade
Asset exposures	Focused on monopolistic and regulated assets	Accepting of assets with some GDP sensitivity	Accepting of assets with GDP sensitivity
Sourcing	Public market, bank intermediated, or direct	Bank intermediated or direct	Bank intermediated or direct
Level of bank competition	Higher	Lower	Lower
Greenfield/brownfield risk	Primarily brownfield	Both	Both
Civenant level	High	High	High
Fixed/floating rate	Mix	Mix	Mix
Co-investing opportunity	Possible	Possible	Possible
Gross IRR	3%–5%	6%–10%	>10%
Investment period (years)	3–5	3–5	3–5
Closed-end fund term (years)	10	10	10

GDP= gross domestic product, IRR = internal rate of return.
Source: Cambridge Associates.

Box 5 *(continued)*

- Despite confined in a range of low risk and return profiles in comparision to equity investments, infrastructure debt funds can thus opt for a variety of strategies in debt investments in terms of type of loan (senior debt, junior debt, and mezzanine); type of loan purchase (in terms of tranches of loans when structured, for instance, by commercial banks); type of lending (direct or secondary); and the type of infrastructure project (in terms of geographies, sectors, and stages). Up to date, the interplay of the multiple stragies resulted in a median net IRR of 7.6% (return) with the underlying standard deviation of 3.4% (risk) (Figure).

Figure: Unlisted Infrastructure: Risk/Return by Primary Strategy (Vintages 2008–2017)*

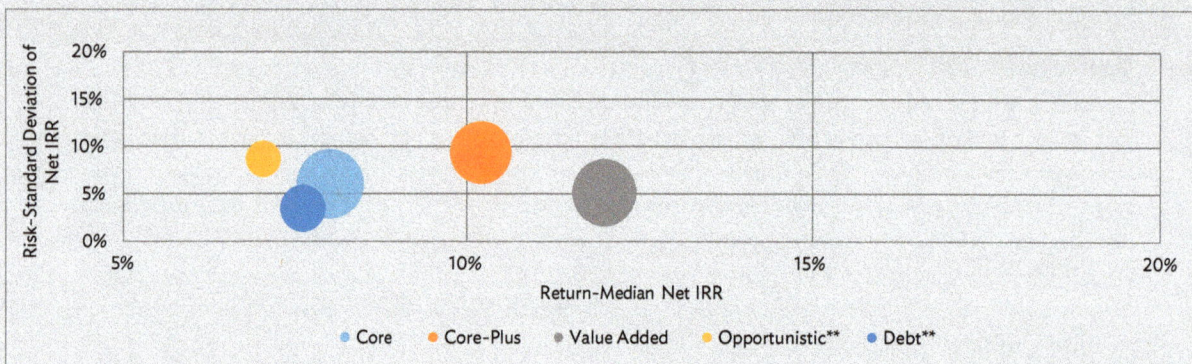

IRR = internal rate of return.

*   The size of each circle represents the capitalization of funds used in the analysis.

** A lower sample size limit was used for these strategies.

Source: Preqin Pro.

Comparing equity strategies (Core, Core-Plus, Value Added, And Opportunistic), infrastructure debt funds present the lowest risk profile with returns between those of opportunistic (7%) and core (8%) strategies. Moreover, infrastructure debt investments have historically experienced lower default rates and higher recoveries than comparable core fixed income. Moody's publishes a periodic analyis on default and recovery rates for project finance bank loans that investigates the performance of global infrastructure loans. The study provides pieces of evidence that infrastructure deals are typically not pro-cyclical and have low default correlations to the broad market and other infrastructure investment.[c]

[a] Debt, Infrastructure Investors (2021).

[b] Cambridge Associates. 2018. Infrastructure debt – Understanding the opportunity.

[c] Moody's. Infrastructure Default and Recovery Rates 1983–2019.

intermediaries waned as for the misalignment of interests between investors and managers.[59] As a result, long-term investors began experimenting with new mechanisms for investing in infrastructure like creating funds management groups, known as captive general partners, as subsidiaries of parent companies (e.g., Allianz Global Investors). The captive general partner structure improved the adjustment between asset holders and asset managers, as the structure was intended for the long-term investor by the long-term investor.

5.2   The Direct Lending Model

In the Global Institutional Investors Outlook recently published by Natixis Investment Managers,[60] the institutional investors surveyed were asked how they prefer to access the private debt market for infrastructure, with 45% opting for direct lending. With direct lending, institutional investors invest in infrastructure loans, which can be either originated by a mandated lead arranger (MLA) bank in a partnership or co-investment, or with a direct origination of infrastructure loans by institutional investors themselves.

In the first model, i.e., the partnership or co-investment model, an institutional investor invests in infrastructure loans originated by an MLA bank and participates in a syndication process (a banks-to-institutional-investors syndicate, as opposed to the more traditional bank-to-bank syndication, see Figure 16) and the MLA bank retains a pre-agreed percentage of each loan in its portfolio. Between 2010 and 2018, many banks entered into partnership agreements with institutional investors (see Box 6 to review some selected examples of partnerships). Partnerships present many advantages, both from the point of view of banks and institutional investors. A partnership creates a captive market for funding; therefore, banks are able to secure funding for infrastructure loans from partner institutional investors. This was particularly critical in the years after the GFC when the appetite for infrastructure debt of nonbank investors was more moderate. From the point of view of institutional investors, partnerships allow investors to build a portfolio of infrastructure loans, relying on the screening and monitoring skills of originating banks, as well as leveraging some services provided by banks, such as rating servicing. At the same time, partnerships present some drawbacks. From the point of view of investors, partnerships limit the deal sourcing to only those projects originated by the partner bank. Given the huge liquidity available among institutional investors and their increasing infrastructure allocations worldwide, after 2018, many banks have dismissed the partnership model, with the possibility to co-invest with several institutional investors in diverse transactions rather than with only a pool of limited selected ones.

The latest trend in debt financing among institutional investors for infrastructure is the direct origination of loans. In this case, it is an institutional investor rather than a bank that lends money directly to the special purpose vehicle (SPV). The direct lending option is confined to a handful of sophisticated investors who have cultivated internal skill development and created internal teams dedicated to infrastructure investment. In some cases, to overcome the lack of specialist investment skills, achieve a higher purchasing power and cost savings, and expand their origination capacity and deal pipeline, a number of institutional investors are adopting collaborative co-investing approaches

---

[59]   On the same point, a research of the OECD noted: "One of the key areas of tension in the unlisted infrastructure equity market has been a conflict of interest between investors and fund managers on fund fees and terms and conditions. The fees charged by managers for core infrastructure have been in the past often excessively high, resembling private equity fees, despite private equity returns being higher" (OECD, 2014a).

[60]   D. Goodsell. 2021 Global Institutional Investors Outlook. Into the great wide open. Natixis Investment Managers.

Figure 16: A Comparison between Traditional Bank Syndicates and Bank-to-Institutional Investors Syndication

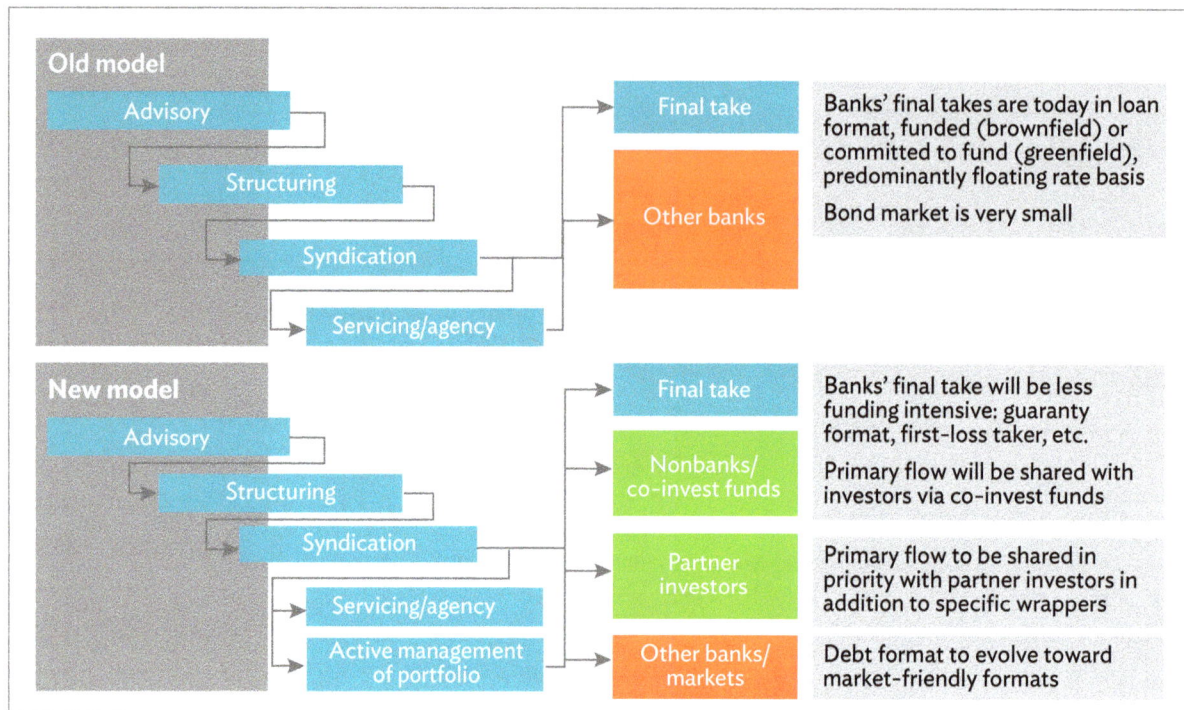

Source: Gatti (2018).

Box 6: Examples of Partnerships between Banks and Institutional Investors for Infrastructure Lending

An example of partnership is represented by the Natixis' Infrastructure Platforms,[a] created in 2012 by the French bank Natixis, with 10 desks worldwide and a team of 100 infrastructure professionals, to provide origination, structuring, and servicing for infrastructure loans to partner institutional investors.

Starting in 2012, Natixis entered into the first partnership agreement with the Belgian insurance company Ageas, one of Europe's 20 largest insurers. Through this partnership, Ageas intended to build a portfolio of €2 billion over a 2–3 year period, while Natixis undertook the servicing of all the loans in the portfolio. Year after year, until 2016, the French bank extended the partnerships under the Natixis' Infrastructure Platforms to a number of institutional investors, including CNP Assurances, MACIF Group (through Zencap Asset Management), and SwissLife, representing a total investment capacity of €4.55 billion in European assets. In 2016, the platform expanded to Asia as KB Insurance. Samsung Life and Samsung Asset Management signed similar cooperation agreements with Natixis, enabling the broadening of the platform to multicurrency investments with a global scope.

The table shows all the partnerships that the French bank created with institutional investors between 2012 and 2016. In all these cooperation agreements with institutional investors, Natixis was in charge of originating and introducing new primary infrastructure transactions to partner investors in agreement with the investment criteria set between the parties (countries, sectors, currencies), while the investors selected the transactions

Box 6 *(continued)*

that they wanted to invest in. Natixis retained a significant portion of each deal on the bank's balance sheet in order to ensure alignment of interest all along the life of the operation and ensured the servicing and administration of all assets in the portfolio.

Table: Partnership Agreements with Institutional Investors Launched under the Natixis' Infrastructure Platforms

Parties Involved in the Partnership Agreement	Year of Inception	Amount of Funding Committed	Scope of the Co-investment	Role of Natixis
Natixis and Ageas	2012	€2 billion	Infrastructure debt	Originator, servicer, account bank, and custodian
Natixis and CNP Assurances	2013	€2 billion	Infrastructure debt	Originator, servicer, and account bank
Natixis and MACIF Group (through Zencap Asset Management)	2014	€250 million	Infrastructure debt	Originator, servicer, account bank, and custodian
Natixis and SwissLife	2015	€300 milion	Infrastructure debt	Originator, servicer, account bank, and custodian
Natixis and KB Insurance	2016	$400 million	Infrastructure and aviation debt	Originator and servicer
Natixis, Samsung Life and Samsung Asset Management	2016	$500 million	Infrastructure debt	Originator and servicer

Source: Natixis. Global Infrastructure and Projects. https://infrastructure.cib.natixis.com/api_website_feature/files/download/847/Triptyque-AEI-2016-numerique-hd.pdf.

Another example of partnership is the Internatioal Finance Corporation (IFC) Managed Co-Lending Portfolio Program (MCPP),[b] which is IFC's groundbreaking syndications platform aimed at creating diversified portfolios of emerging market infrastructure loans, allowing institutional investors to increase exposure to this asset class. The IFC MCPP allows institutional investors the opportunity to passively participate in IFC's future loan portfolio. The program is designed for investors that do not have the capacity to invest on a "deal-by-deal" basis and that decide to provide capital on a portfolio basis.

One of the first partners of the IFC MCPP Program was the People's Bank of China in 2013. The People's Bank of China, through the State Administration for Foreign Exchange, committed $3 billion under the platform to be invested over a 6-year period. Over the years, IFC has welcomed several more partners to the MCPP, including Allianz Global Investors in 2016, Eastspring Investments, the Hong Kong Monetary Authority, Liberty Specialty Markets, and Munich Re in 2017; and AXA and Swiss Re in 2018.

[a] Natixis. Our Infrastructure Solutions Comprehensive Solutions Offering Based On Extensive Track Record.
[b] IFC. Managed Co-Lending Portfolio Program.

to directly deploy debt capital into infrastructure.[61] These co-investment initiatives are independent from external fund managers and MLA banks, and instead rely on like-minded peer institutional investors.

Anecdotal evidence indicates that M&G Prudential originated a £266 million senior loan to student housing projects in London and it committed £290 million funding for a hospital facility in Northwest England. Another example includes Generali Global Infrastructure, which in 2020 received formal authorization by the Italian Central Bank to operate in direct lending to infrastructure. The company will invest in themes such as energy transition, renewable energy, green mobility, digital transition, and social infrastructure. As an example of peer-to-peer platform for direct lending, Pensions Infrastructure Platform is a dedicated infrastructure investment manager established by 10 large-pension schemes in the United Kingdom (UK) to facilitate long-term investment into UK infrastructure. Even if mainly focused on infrastructure equity investments, Pensions Infrastructure Platform completed the first direct lending transaction in 2014, providing £27.5 million of debt financing to fund a portfolio of 2,366 rooftop solar assets in England and Wales. Another example of peer-to-peer platform is the Climate Finance Leadership Initiative in India, which involves different institutional investors, including Allianz Global Investors, AXA, Bloomberg, Enel, Goldman Sachs, Japan's Government Pension Investment Fund, HSBC, and Macquarie; and engages with the Government of India and the multilateral community to invest in renewable energy projects in India.

5.3   The Securitization Model

Since the collapse of Lehman Brothers in late 2008, the market for securitization has been undergoing a dramatic downward trend.[62] Still today, most securitizations are launched for generating collateral to be used for refinancing at central banks rather than to place securities with institutional investors. It comes as no surprise, then, that the market for securitization of infrastructure loans in the form of project finance collateralized loan obligations (CLOs) or collateralized debt obligations almost disappeared after 2008. However, in more recent years, the resurgence of the originate-to-distribute model has raised interest in the securitization model by institutional investors,[63] with a handful of project finance CLOs closed in the past 5 years (Box 7 provides information on some of these deals involving securitizations of CLO for infrastructure lending or project finance).

As shown in Figure 17, a CLO is a transaction that involves repackaging the risk of a portfolio of financial assets. This risk is passed on to an SPV, either by transferring the portfolio to the SPV (cash securitization), or using credit derivative techniques (synthetic securitization, when risk is transferred through bundled loans via credit derivatives or guarantees). The risk is then sold to the capital markets by way of securities issued by the SPV. These securities are rated by credit rating agencies according to their seniority within the capital structure. A broad range of investor groups

---

61   This collaborative co-investment approach among institutional investors is very similar to what happens in equity investments, as reported in R. Della Croce and R. Sharma. 2014. *Pooling of Institutional Investors Capital: Selected case studies in unlisted equity infrastructure*, OECD.

62   In Europe, for example, the securitization market has dropped from the €450 billion of pre-crisis years (2006–2007) to €108 billion as at the end of 2019. AFME Finance for Europe. 2020. *Capital Markets Union. Key Performance Indicators – Third Edition*.

63   J. Grushkin and D. Bartfeld. 2013. Securitizing Project Finance Loans: Are PF CLOs Poised for a Comeback? *The Journal of Structured Finance Fall.19 (3). pp. 76–81.*

Box 7: Examples of Project Finance Collateralized Loan Obligations for Infrastructure

Project finance collateralized loan obligations closed before the global financial crisis, 1998–2009

The table reports the transaction records of 11 project finance collateralized loan obligations (CLOs) closed in the period between 1998 and 2009. Credit Suisse First Boston (CSFB) finalized the first CLO transaction backed by project finance loans in March 1998 (Project Funding Corp. I). Notes were backed by assigned interest in a pool of 41 fully funded amortizing project finance loans purchased from CSFB's loan portfolio. Each of the loans was a floating rate United States (US) dollar-denominated term loan secured by a US domestic project (with the exception of one Chilean project). Between 1999 and 2001, there were two other cash CLOs backed by project loans originated by Citigroup and CSFB. In August 2001, the TCW Group, majority-owned by Société Générale Asset Management, launched Global Project Fund I (GPF I). This fund, with a 3-year life span, pooled investments in 14 projects including a gas-to-liquid methanol project financing in Western Australia and a power project in the Dominican Republic. Three years later, TCW recapitalized its original $500 million GPF and increased the equity and debt investment limit in the new fund to $700 million. This fund, called Global Project Fund II (GPF II), first bought out the assets of the original fund; the remaining proceeds were then used to acquire additional emerging markets' power assets over a 5-year investment period.

Table: Project Finance Collateralized Loan Obligations Closed in 1998–2009

Transaction	Year	Size (million)	Risk	Originator	Key Features
Project Fund Corp I	1998	$617	True Sales	CSFB	41 PF loans; infrastructure projects located in the US (only one project in Chile)
TCW GPF I	2001	$500	True Sales	TCW Group	14 PF loans; infrastructure projects including a gas-to-liquid methanol project in Western Australia and a power project in the Dominican Republic
TCW GPF II	2004	$700	True Sales	TCW Group	Transfer of the 14 PF loans of the TCW GPF I fund; the remaining proceeds used to acquire additional PF loans backed by emerging-markets power assets
EPIC I	2004	£392	Synthetic	Depfa Bank	Risk transfer for 8 PF loans backed by the UK. PFI/PPP projects in publicly regulated areas
EPIC II	2005	€900	Synthetic	Depfa Bank	Risk transfer for a global portfolio of PFI loans and bonds
TCW GPF III	2005	$1,500	True Sales	TCW Group	15 PF loans and credit-linked notes; GPF III's notes were listed on the Irish stock exchange
Stichting PROFILE	2005	£383	Synthetic	SMBC–NIBC	Risk transfer for PF loans backed by the UK PFI/PPP projects, mainly in the hospital and education area; the deal involved KfW as a zero-weighted swap counterparty
WISE	2006	£1,500	Synthetic	Dexia	Portfolio of wrapped bonds related to PPP/PFI and regulated utilities in the water, electricity and gas sectors
SMART PFI	2007	£400	Synthetic	SMBC	Risk transfer for PF loans backed by the UK PFI/PPP projects mainly in the hospital and education area; the deal involved KfW as a zero-weighted swap counterparty
BACCHUS 2008-2	2008	€453	True Sales	IKB	68 PF loans secured by infrastructure projects and PFI/PPPs mainly in the UK and Spain

continued on next page

Box 7 *(continued)*

Transaction	Year	Size (million)	Risk	Originator	Key Features
Adriana Infrastructure CLO I	2008	£1,018	True Sales	NIBC	Portfolio of PF loans secured by the UK and non-UK PFI/PPPs, both greenfield and brownfield
Boadilla PF CLO I	2009	€102	Synthetic	Banco Santander	Risk transfer for PF loans backed by renewable energy projects in the solar and wind sectors, mainly located in Spain

CLO = collateralized loan obligation, PF = project finance, PFI/PPP = private finance initiative/public–private partnership, UK = United Kingdom, US = United States.
Source: Buscaino et al. (2012), based on Fitch Ratings, Standard & Poor's, and Moody's pre-sale reports.

It was not until November 2004 that the first synthetic deal appeared in Europe, when Depfa Bank launched Essential Public Infrastructure Capital (EPIC). This deal achieved capital relief via a £392 million synthetic securitization of a portfolio of the UK private finance initiative/public–private partnership (PFI/PPP) loans in an offering led by Merrill Lynch. In the summer of 2005, Depfa Bank returned with a second EPIC deal, this time backed by a €900 million global portfolio of PFI loans and bonds, once again managed by Merrill Lynch. In August 2005, TCW closed its $1.5 billion Global Project Fund III (GPF III). At close, funded proceeds from GPF III were used to purchase 15 project finance loans and credit-linked notes whose underlying obligations constituted similar loans.

During the 5-year investment period of TCW's GPF III, the remaining commitments were to be used to fund additional project finance loans under a revolving note tranche and equity. Interestingly, assets were not completely known at closing, a significant level of risk for investors. However, since the investment criteria included limitations on exposure to obligor, country, region, and industry, each project finance loan was required to have a minimum credit rating of BB from Standard & Poor's. Unlike its two predecessors, GPF III's notes were listed as asset-backed debt securities on the Irish stock exchange. In November 2005, the £383 million Stichting Profile Securitization I, also driven by regulatory capital considerations, came to market. The deal was a partnership between Sumitomo Mitsui Banking Corporation and NIB Capital (who acted as lead arranger on the deal). Late in 2006, Dexia entered the market with its WISE transaction, backed by a portfolio of wrapped bonds.

Finally, in March 2007 SMBC launched the Smart PFI 2007 deal. In April 2008, NIBC Bank NV, as originator of a £1 billion project finance/PPP portfolio, entered into a servicing and collateral management agreement with Adriana Infrastructure CLO I. The issuing vehicle guaranteed the payment of the notes' principal and interest with a mixed portfolio of the UK and non-UK PPPs. The underlying projects were a variety of greenfield and brownfield initiatives. In December 2008, Bacchus PLC was set up by IKB Deutsche Industriebank AG to sell a €453 million mixed portfolio of 68 infrastructure project and PPP loans. IKB acted as servicer for the transaction. Most of the projects were located in Spain and the UK. Finally, in December 2009, the synthetic CLO Boadilla PF CLO 2009-I was set up by Banco Santander to transfer the risk of a €102 million project finance loan portfolio composed of renewable energy projects in the solar and wind sectors, mainly located in Spain.

In 2012, Buscaino et al.a used these projects to study the determinants of the spread of project finance CLOs and understand the most influential determinants of the pricing of such transactions. Their findings indicate that, together with rating, the nature of the underlying assets had a substantial impact on CLO pricing,

Box 7 (*continued*)

showing that primary market spread was significantly higher when the underlying project finance loans bore a higher level of market risk as compared to issues backed by projects with low market risk exposure. The larger proportion of projects still under construction in the securitized portfolio was another feature that explained the at-issue spread.

Project finance collateralized loan obligations closed in recent years

The next table reports the transaction records of eight project finance CLOs closed in the past 5 years. RIN, a managed $431.3 million project finance CLO with project finance loans originated by RREEF America, the real estate investment unit of Deutsche Asset Management, was issued in 2017 with three classes of notes through Barclays as lead underwriter. Class A tranche carried an Aaa rating from Moody's and benefited from a 39.3% effective subordination of the $49.6 million series of Class B notes (rated Aa3), the $55 million in Class C notes (Baa3), and an unrated tranche of preferred shares totaling $64.7 million, that were retained by RREEF. The CLO was structured so that project finance loan investments could represent 45% of the portfolio in the contracted or merchant thermal electricity sector, up to 30% in large infrastructure transactions or up to 15% in the regulated assets/utilities sector. Between 2017 and 2018, there were two synthetic CLOs backed by project finance loans originated by Banco Santander. In 2017, with Renew Project Finance CLO 2017-1, the Spanish Group transferred the risk related to a €2.3 billion portfolio of project finance loans. The reference pool was static and comprised 241 project finance loans related to renewable energy; transport; social infrastructure; and technology, media, and telecommunications, located in France, Germany, Portugal, Spain, and other European Union countries.

Table: Project Finance Collateralized Loan Obligations Closed in 2017–2021

Transaction	Year	Size (million)	Risk	Originator	Key Features
RIN Ldt.	2017	$431.3	True Sales	RREEF America	Portfolio of PF loans backed by utility and infrastructure projects in the US
Renew Project Finance CLO 2017-1	2017	€2,300	Synthetic	Banco Santander	Risk transfer for 241 PF loans related to renewable energy, transport, social infrastructure and telecommunications, mainly located in Spain, Portugal, France, and Germany
Fitzroy 2018-1	2018	€1,120	Synthetic	Banco Santander	Risk transfer for a portfolio of PF loans related to projects in the UK in the renewable energy, PPP/PFI, and utility sector
Room2Run	2018	$1,000	Synthetic	African Development Bank	Risk transfer for 50 PF loans related to power and transportation infrastructure in Africa
Bayfront Infrastructure Capital Pte. Ltd.	2018	$458	True Sales	Multiple originators	37 PF loans related to 30 projects across Asia and Pacific and the Middle East
Bayfront Infrastructure Capital II Pte. Ltd.	2021	$401,2	True Sales	Multiple originators	27 PF loans related to 25 projects in Asia and Pacific, the Middle East, and South America
SPV Project 2011	2021	€25.6	True Sales	Glennmont Partners	Portfolio of PF loans related to renewable energy projects in Southern Italy
STWD Investment Management	2021	$500	True Sales	MUFG	Portfolio of PF loans related to energy infrastructure projects in the US

CLO = collateralized loan obligation, PF = project finance, PFI/PPP = private finance initiative/public–private partnership, SPV = special purpose vehicle, UK = United Kingdom, US = United States.
Source: Scope Ratings, Refinitiv, Dealogic Deal Intelligence.

Box 7 *(continued)*

In 2018, another synthetic project finance CLO was closed by the Spanish Group, transferring the risk of a €1.12 billion portfolio of project finance loans. The UK loans made up 97% of the initial portfolio, with renewable energy at roughly 50%, PPP/PFI at 30%, utilities 13%, and infrastructure 8%. Most projects in the initial portfolio benefited from stable and predictable cash flows, directly or indirectly linked to the UK government for 69% of the initial balance. In the same year, an additional synthetic project finance CLO, Room2Run, transferred the mezzanine credit risk on a $1 billion portfolio of approximately 45 project finance loans originated by the African Development Bank, including power and transportation infrastructure in North Africa, West Africa, Central Africa, East Africa, and Southern Africa. Mariner, the global alternative asset manager and a majority-owned subsidiary of ORIX USA, acted as the lead investor in the transaction through its International Infrastructure Finance Company II fund (IIFC II). Africa50, the pan-African infrastructure investment platform, invested alongside Mariner in the private sector tranche. Additional credit protection was provided by the European Commission's European Fund for Sustainable Development in the form of a senior mezzanine guarantee. Again in 2018, Bayfront Infrastructure raised $458 million in its inaugural project finance CLO (Bayfront Infrastructure Capital), secured by cash flows from a portfolio of 37 syndicated senior project finance loans to 30 projects originated by multiple international and regional banks (whose names are undisclosed) across Asia and Pacific and the Middle East. Only after a few years, in early 2021, Bayfront Infrastructure launched a second securitization of project finance loans (Bayfront Infrastructure Capital II), backed by a $401.2 million portfolio of bank-syndicated senior secured project finance loans to projects in Asia and Pacific, the Middle East, and South America in energy-related sectors such as power generation renewables and nonrenewables, and oil and gas.

Box 8 expands the analysis of these CLO transactions launched by Bayfront Infrastructure, as they are relevant for three main reasons: first, their geographical scope focuses on Asia; second, they are unique cases of multi-originator platforms, pooling together securitized loans originated by many different international and regional banks; and lastly, the deal prospectuses are publicly available, providing extensive information on the deals. Other recent CLO projects closed in 2021 include SPV Project 2011 and STWD 2021-SIF1. In SPV Project 2011, the asset manager Glennmont Partners, through its Renewable Energy Backed Securities credit fund, completed the issuance of a €25.6 million green asset-backed securities portfolio of Italian renewable energy plants totaling 110 megawatts (MW). The deal was split between €16.5 million in Class A asset-backed floating-rate notes, and €9.1 million of Class B asset-backed floating-rate and variable return notes. The proceeds were used to refinance Glennmont's acquisition of project finance loan agreements from a mid size Italian bank used to finance the 110 MW wind and solar portfolio. STWD 2021-SIF1 was closed by Starwood Property Trust and backed by a pool of $500 million long-term, critical, core energy infrastructure project finance loans originated by the Japanese MUFG Bank.

---

[a] V. Buscaino et al. 2012. Project Finance Collateralised Debt Obligations: An Empirical Analysis of Spread Determinants. *European Financial Management*. 18 (5). pp. 950–969.

purchase the securities based on their individual risk/return preferences and investment criteria. An asset manager typically manages the underlying pool of loans by constructing a portfolio and optimizing portfolio performance. Investors in the securities bear the risk of losses suffered by the portfolio. Thus, under a CLO structure, capital market notes are paid by cash flows generated from a pool of project finance loans or bonds. The whole transaction benefits from this scheme because the credit strength of the notes will generally be stronger than the credit strength of any individual project loan, due to the fact that pooled cash flows diversify default risk. Compared to an ordinary CLO deal, where collateral consists of a mix of loans, bonds, and other types of securities, in project finance CLOs the collateral is represented only by a portfolio of project finance loans.

Figure 17: Typical Structure of a Project Finance Collateralized Loan Obligation

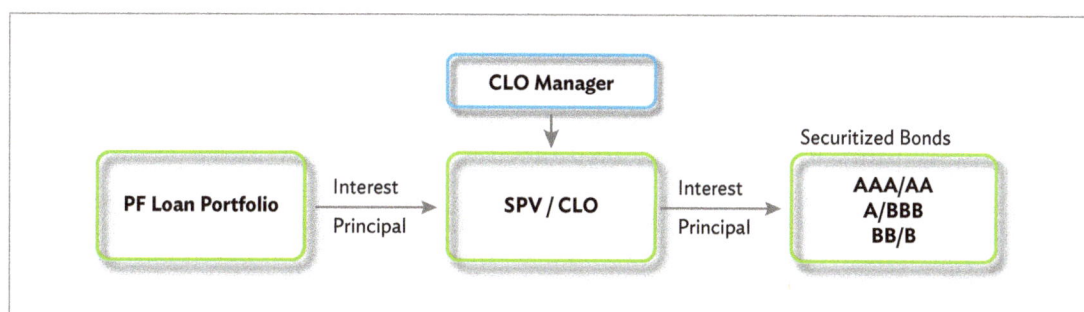

CLO = collateralized loan obligation, PF = project finance, SPV = special purpose vehicle.
Source: Authors.

The basic difference between the securitization of project finance loans and the partnership or co-investment model is that in the latter the institutional investor becomes one of the parties lending directly to the SPV. Instead, with securitizations, investors participate in a pool of loans (in other words, financing the infrastructure project only indirectly) originated by a bank. From an institutional investor's perspective, the advantage of this model is that these kinds of loans structured as bonds can be tailored to their specific needs, and they can benefit from a diversified default risk. From a bank's perspective, by moving project finance loans from the bank balance sheets and transferring the credit risk of the underlying loan portfolio to bond investors via securitization, project finance CLOs accelerate loan issuance, and free up bank lending capacity (i.e., asset recycling), thereby expanding overall lending to infrastructure.[64]

---

[64] G20 Sustainable Finance Working Group. 2018. *Towards a Sustainable Infrastructure Securitisation Market: The Role of Collateralised Loan Obligations (CLO).*

Box 8: Project Finance Collateralized Loan Obligation Targeting Institutional Investors to Diversify Asian Infrastructure Financing: The Case of Bayfront Infrastructure Capital

Short description of the transaction

Clifford Capital, a Singapore-based specialist arranger and provider of project and asset-backed finance solutions, whose shareholders include the Asian Development Bank, designed and structured a $458 million project finance collateralized loan obligation (CLO) transaction (Bayfront Infrastructure Capital) aimed at mobilizing institutional capital for infrastructure debt in Asia and Pacific and the Middle East. The project finance CLO transaction transferred 37 project finance loans from international and regional banks to institutional investors. The transaction was designed to provide institutional investors, who have historically had limited access to high-quality infrastructure debt through the capital markets in the Asia and Pacific and the Middle East regions, with exposure to a diversified portfolio of project and infrastructure loans.[a]

The offering was met with strong demand from institutional investors, including insurers, asset managers, pension funds, and endowment funds. The success of this first CLO transaction allowed Clifford Capital to launch a second CLO, backed by a $401.2 million portfolio of 27 project finance loans, which was priced in June 2021 (Bayfront Infrastructure Capital II).

Overview of the portfolio

The portfolio of project finance loans was selected and constituted by Clifford Capital and sourced from multiple originators, which are all leading international and regional banks. The portfolio was made to be broadly representative of the geographical and sector activity in the infrastructure and project finance industry across Asia and Pacific and the Middle East. As shown in the figure, the portfolio of 37 project finance loans is diversified across 30 projects spread among eight industry subsectors, with a focus on infrastructure assets in the conventional power and water, renewable power, transportation infrastructure, energy, and shipping subsectors.

Figure: Portfolio by Sector

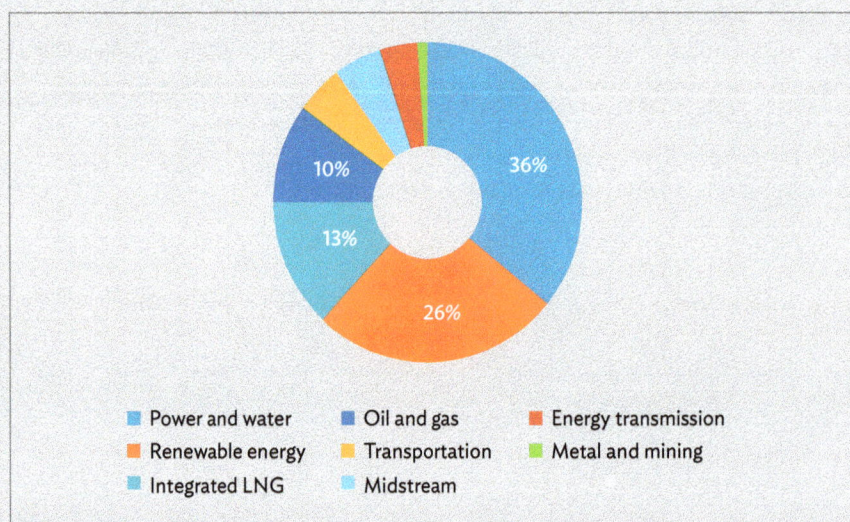

LNG = liquefied natural gas.
Source: Bayfront Infrastructure Capital investor reports

Box 8 *(continued)*

The projects underlying the portfolio are located in 16 countries across the rapidly growing Asia and Pacific and Middle East regions are shown in the next figure.

Figure: Portfolio by Country of Project

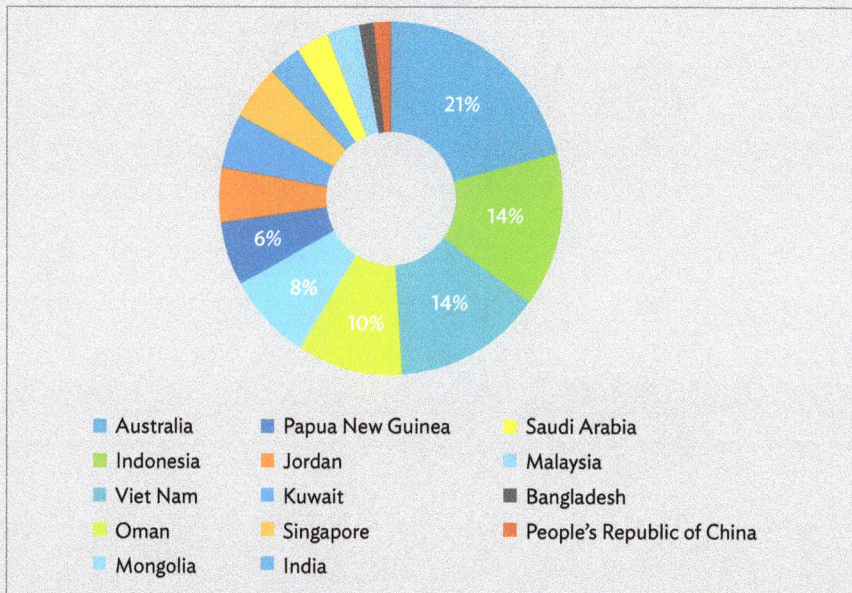

Source: Bayfront Infrastructure Capital investor reports.

As shown in the next figure, 75.6% of the portfolio relates to operational projects, while the remaining 24.4% relates to underlying projects that are in advanced stages of construction, but which benefit from credit mitigants, such as sovereign and sponsor completion guarantees, which substantially mitigates the construction or completion risk that may affect the cash flows and longer-term performance of the portfolio.

Figure: Portfolio by Construction Risk

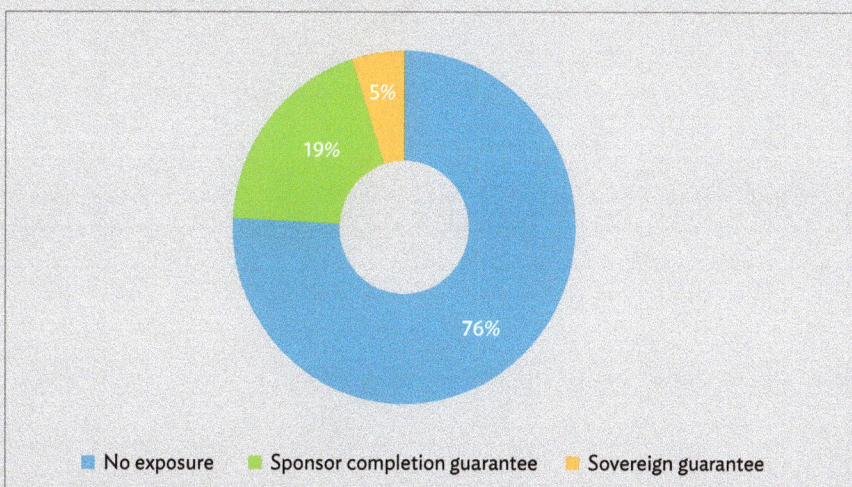

Source: Bayfront Infrastructure Capital investor reports.

Box 8 *(continued)*

In addition, as shown in the next figure, 38.2% of the portfolio is supported by collateral obligations provided by export credit agencies and multilateral financial institutions through various forms of credit enhancement such as preferred creditor status, guarantees, and insurance. The involvement of these export credit agencies and multilateral financial institutions helps to mitigate political and commercial risks relating to each of the underlying projects.

Figure: Portfolio by Credit Enhancement

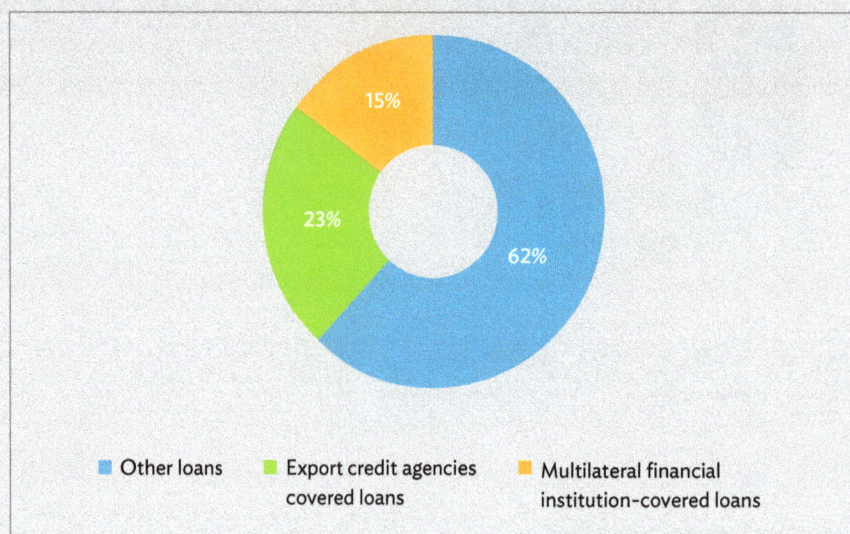

Source: Bayfront Infrastructure Capital investor reports.

Collateralized loan obligation notes issuance and key transaction parties involved
Under the CLO structure, four classes of notes were issued on 31 July 2018. The Class A Notes, Class B Notes, and Class C Notes were rated by Moody's and listed on the Singapore Exchange. The issuer was Bayfront Infrastructure Capital Pte. Ltd., while the sponsor was Clifford Capital Pte. Ltd. The Subordinated Notes were solely subscribed by Clifford Capital as sponsor and manager of the transaction. By taking on a subordinated 10% first-loss piece of the capital structure, Clifford provided investors with comfort and confidence in the securities.

As sponsor, Clifford Capital was responsible for the sourcing of the project finance loans from the originating banks, including initial screening, credit analysis, due diligence, and documentation. Deutsche Bank AG Singapore Branch was appointed as the transaction administrator to perform certain portfolio administration and reporting services, while Citigroup and Standard Chartered Bank as joint global coordinators, joint bookrunners, and joint lead managers. Joint bookrunners and lead managers also included SMBC Nikko, HSBC, and DBS.

Both the loans and the notes were denominated in US dollars and pay floating-rate interest payments linked to US dollar London interbank offered rate (LIBOR).

The table reports the details regarding the classes of notes, the amount issued, their rating, spread, and maturity date.

Box 8 *(continued)*

Table: Classes of Notes, Amount Issued, Rating, Spread, and Maturity Date

Class of Shares	Amount Issued ($ million)	Amount Outstanding as of Oct 2021 ($ million)	Issue Ratings (Moody's)		Spread over 6 months LIBOR	Maturity Date
			Original	Current		
A	320.6	124.4	Aaa (sf)	Aaa (sf)	145 bps	11-Jan-38
B	72.6	72.6	Aa3 (sf)	Aa1 (sf)	195 bps	11-Jan-38
C	19.0	19.0	Baa3 (sf)	A3 (sf)	315 bps	11-Jan-38
Subordinated	45.8	45.8	Not rated	Not rated	n.a.	11-Jan-38

bps = basis points, n.a. = not applicable, LIBOR = London interbank offered rate.
Source: Bayfront Infrastructure Capital offering circular.

Investor profiles

The deal catalyzed interest from different institutional investors, including insurers, asset managers, pension funds and endowment funds, as shown in the next figure. Subscriber investors are mainly located in the Asia and Pacific region, but they also include investors from Europe and the Middle East.

Key results and lessons learned

Clifford Capital successfully launched Asia's first infrastructure project finance CLO, with an issue size of $458 million. The transaction enhanced banks' ability to originate, arrange, and provide infrastructure project financing within the region, while providing institutional investors access to high-quality infrastructure debt in Asia and Pacific and the Middle East.

Figure: Investor Profiles by Type and Geographic Location

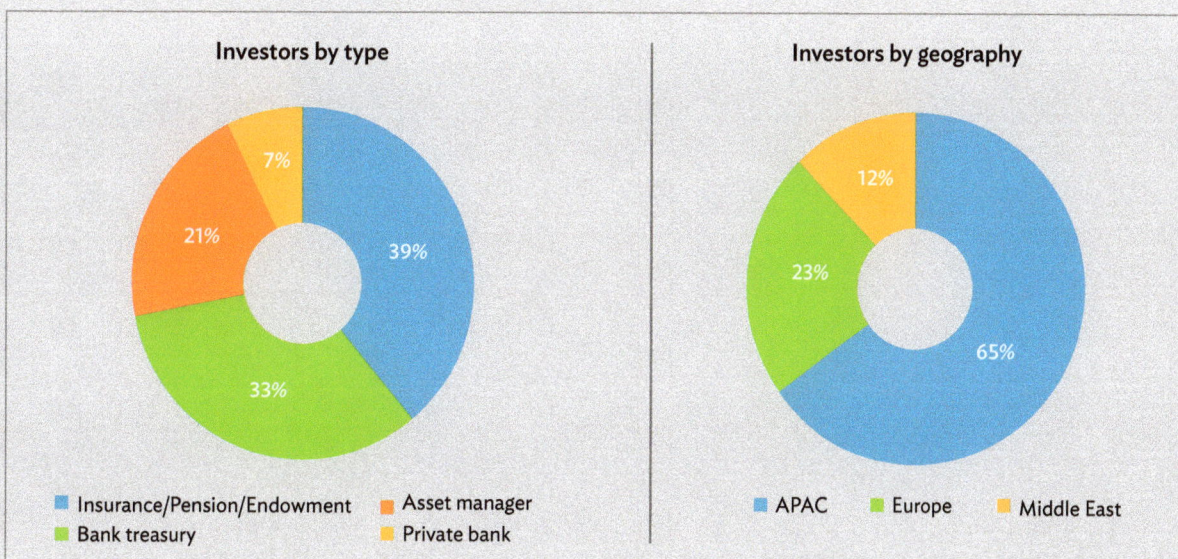

Source: Bayfront Infrastructure Capital investor reports.

Box 8 *(continued)*

The transaction can be regarded as a successful example of project finance CLO for a number of reasons:

- Clifford Capital carefully mitigated the level of risk by securitizing loans on projects that were already operational or close to completion; in addition, various forms of credit enhancement on the projects were available to reduce the risk borne by institutional investors.

- Bayfront Infrastructure Capital served as multi-originator platform, therefore reducing the risk by increasing the project finance loan portfolio diversification, not only in terms of infrastructure projects, sectors and geographies, but also in terms of originating banks.

- Confidence in the transaction was raised by Clifford Capital taking on a subordinated 10% first-loss piece of the capital structure.

- Notes were denominated in US dollars and the interest rate was linked to LIBOR; denominating securities in a commonly used currency and tying interest rates to a well-known benchmark helped mitigate currency and interest-rate risk.

[a] All the information and data reported in the case description and analysis were sourced from the documents publicly available in the Bayfront Infrastructure Capital investor report (https://www.bayfront.sg/bic1).

Source: Bayfront Infrastructure Capital investor report.

6

THE ROLE OF THE PUBLIC SECTOR AND MULTILATERAL DEVELOPMENT BANKS

Despite the huge private liquidity available and the increasing appeal of infrastructure to institutional investors due to the ideal match between their risk-and-return profile and the characteristics of infrastructure as an asset class, the uptake of these investors has been relatively small. According to a recent survey by the OECD, they typically commit only a small portion, around 2%–3% on average, of their total assets to unlisted infrastructure.[65] In particular, investors seem to prefer investment in developed markets, which are considered to have more stable political systems and reliable legal frameworks, compared to developing economies. The current level of institutional investor activity in new infrastructure deals for both debt and equity investments is extremely low, at only 0.7% of total private participation in infrastructure investment in developing economies, with bank loans the most prominent funding source.[66] With particular reference to Asia and Pacific, institutional investors see the opportunity of investing in the area, given that the majority of infrastructure investment is coming from there; however, they remain skeptical over the long-term fundamentals of the Asia and Pacific infrastructure sector (footnote 34). After the pandemic, these investors are expected to decrease their commitment to infrastructure investment in Asia, while development finance institutions (DFIs) and multilateral development banks (MDBs) are expected to increase funding for the development of infrastructure in the region (Table 4).

Table 4: Most Suitable Sources of Financial Investment for Asia and Pacific Infrastructure, 2019 versus 2020 (% of respondents)

	2019	2020
Pension funds	70%	48%
Development finance institutions	24%	38%
Multilateral development banks	n.a.	37%
Local commercial banks	27%	27%
International commercial banks	34%	23%
Sovereign wealth funds	14%	18%
Export credit agencies	8%	15%

n.a. = not applicable.
a   As per % of respondents, excluding India and the People's Republic of China.
Source: White & Case LLP, 2021.

One of the main challenges in attracting institutional investors to infrastructure is the level of risk that applies across the whole infrastructure life cycle. Vecchi et al. (2017)[67] provided a classification of all the risks that affect infrastructure projects according to the project development phase.

[65]   OECD. 2021. Annual Survey of Large Pension Funds and Public Pension Reserve Funds.
[66]   Swiss Re Group. 2020. Closing the Infrastructure Gap: Mobilising Institutional Investment into Sustainable, Quality Infrastructure in Emerging Markets and Developing Economies (EMDEs).
[67]   V. Vecchi et al. 2017. Government Policies to Enhance Access to Credit for Infrastructure-based PPPs: An Approach to Classification and Appraisal. *Public Money & Management.* 37 (2). pp. 133-140.

Among others, the most relevant risks are political and regulatory risks, construction and land expropriation risks, and demand risks. These risks are particularly applicable to greenfield projects in emerging economies, areas in which institutional investors are more reluctant to invest, as demonstrated by the latest figures regarding institutional investment activities. In the wake of the pandemic, in 2020, 85% of total capital committed to unlisted infrastructure focused on developed markets, for their more stable political and regulatory environment. Furthermore, out of 90 pension funds investing in infrastructure surveyed in 2020 by the OECD, only 17 were keen to invest in greenfield projects, while the rest invested only in brownfield projects (footnote 65).

In this context, given the salient role of infrastructure for a sustainable post-pandemic recovery, and the importance of private capital to close the infrastructure gap, governments, DFIs, and MDBs play a key role to attract larger volumes of institutional investors' capital into infrastructure projects. Governments and MDBs can influence the magnitude of risks related to infrastructure projects and/or reduce the probability of their occurrence, by acting at both the project and system levels.

First, governments can influence political and regulatory risks by creating a more conducive institutional environment, including making credible commitments to honor the terms of the agreement, and develop clear and reliable estimates on development and construction costs, tariff, and demand definition and trends. This may entail the following:

- A stable long-term plan for infrastructure development; enhanced certainty and acceptance of novel approaches to infrastructure development (for example PPP, privatization, or pure private development); enhanced transparency and accuracy of the infrastructure pipeline; reliability of feasibility studies; and credible commitment to providing necessary permissions.

- The creation of confidence in rules about, among other things, public procurement, permits, expropriation, taxation, litigation, and tariffs.

A growing body of literature has demonstrated the importance of a favorable institutional environment to sustain infrastructure financing (see, among other things, the 2015 study by Verhoest, Petersen, Scherrer, and Soecipto).[68] Also, investors surveys[69] have shown that the majority of institutional investors considers the robustness of the rule of law, regulation, bidding process, and track record of a country as decisive guiding factors for asset allocation, which clearly demonstrates the importance of these institutional factors for private investors. A favorable institutional environment should include a clear infrastructure policy, an appropriate legal and regulatory framework, and dedicated supporting institutions to create a pipeline of bankable infrastructure projects.

Even if this is not the focus of the report, the key steps to develop a pipeline of well-structured and bankable infrastructure projects can be summarized as follows:[70]

- Managing a rigorous project preparation process: assemble an experienced, cross-functional infrastructure task force and secure the buy-in and leadership of

---

[68]   K. Verhoest et al. 2015. How Do Governments Support the Development of Public Private Partnerships? Measuring and Comparing PPP Governmental Support in 20 European Countries. *Transport Reviews*. 35(2). pp. 118–139.

[69]   See for example: Allen & Overy. Institutional Investor Forum 2021: How I made it.

[70]   See also: World Economic Forum. 2013. Strategic Infrastructure. Steps to Prepare and Accelerate Public-Private Partnerships.

high-level political champions and public servants; establish a well-defined governance structure, involving all key stakeholders with clear roles and responsibilities; ensure sufficient up-front funds for project preparation; and establish dedicated facilities for feasibility study and project development;

- Conducting robust financial feasibility studies: follow a structured approach to estimate the demand that the facility is going to attract and the optimal technical scope and specification, determine the revenue sources for the project and its commercial attractiveness for private bidders, pursue stakeholder buy-in, and expedite legal requirements such as permits and land acquisition;

- Structuring a balanced risk allocation to increase bankability and attract institutional investors.

In addition, governments, DFIs, and MDBs can introduce specific measures to mitigate the risk profile of infrastructure, to expand lending at project level. These measures are particularly helpful to support direct lending provided by institutional investors to the SPV, either directly in a co-investment with banks or through an intermediary asset manager, as discussed in Section 5.

These measures may be based on five different mechanisms (Vecchi et al. [2017]) (footnote 68):

(i) Grants, such as lump-sum grants, to reduce the capital requirements of the project, revenue grants to integrate revenues, or grants on debt interests to reduce operating costs.

(ii) Availability-based payments, to neutralize the demand risk while leaving the construction and performance risk with the SPV.

(iii) Credit enhancement, to reduce or cancel the credit default risk for lenders; credit enhancement tools can assume three main forms:

   ° Minimum revenue guarantee to reduce the demand risk, which is partially retained by the public contracting authority, which is committed to guarantee a certain level of revenues, generally those necessary to cover the debt service at some level of the debt service cover ratio.

   ° Guarantee in case of default, which pays debt principal and interest in the case of the SPV's default.

   ° Guarantee in case of refinancing, which repays lenders if the SPV fails to refinance the loan at maturity; indeed in the context of mini perm (i.e., a debt structure that can— "soft" mini perm or must "hard" mini perm— be refinanced after the construction phase), there is a risk that existing debt will not be repaid from new borrowing (risk of refinancing), especially in case of increased interest rates or adversely changed market conditions.

(iv) Direct provision of debt and equity capital by government, public financial agencies, or development banks, to offset the liquidity gap; this provision can take three main forms:

   ° Subordinated (junior) debt aimed at enhancing the credit quality of the senior debt in order to attract investment from insurance companies, pension funds, and other institutional investors.

° Debt, provided at market conditions or at lower interest rate, to help the project to meet the expectation of debt capital investors, in terms of interest rate, debt service cover ratio, and maturity.

° Equity, provided at market conditions or at more advantageous conditions, to fill the equity gap and to reduce the financial gearing, therefore reducing the exposure to credit risk for private lenders.

(v) Other measures, among them, favorable taxation.

Table 5 presents the different alternatives to support institutional investors' lending to infrastructure projects, and their effects on the main components of a project capital structure and cash flow. Some of these measures can be considered a way to expand lending at project level, by acting on the capital structure to increase the availability of funding during the pre-completion or construction phase. Other measures instead are intended to provide support in the post-completion or operational phase, by offering stabilization to the project cash flow.

Table 5: Main Instruments to Support Lending to Infrastructure-Based Public–Private Partnership Projects

Measures	Features	Effects on Capital Structure/ Cash Flow	Pre-Completion Phase Measure	Post-Completion Phase Measure
1. Grant	1.1 Lump-sum capital grant	Reducing the need for private capital.	X	
	1.2 Revenue grant: 1.2.1 Periodic fixed amount (mitigating the demand risk) 1.2.2 Revenue integration (it leaves the demand risk on the private player)	Mitigating the demand risk; increasing the revenue volume and stability (when the SPV retains the demand risk and tariffs are set at socially acceptable levels).		X
	1.3 Grant on debt interests	Decreasing the overall financial costs by reducing the amount of interest due to the debt provider.		X
2. Availability payment	2. Availability payment is typical in the social infrastructure sector, where the main user is the public sector. In some cases, availability payment can be used also for economic infrastructure, in which case the service can be delivered free of charge to users or tariffs are collected by the public authority.	Eliminating the demand risk; ensuring the revenue stability.		X

continued on next page

Table 5 *(continued)*

Measures	Features	Effects on Capital Structure/ Cash Flow	Pre-Completion Phase Measure	Post-Completion Phase Measure
3. Guarantee on debt	3.1 Minimum revenue guarantee, to guarantee a minimum level of revenues (generally those necessary to cover the debt service at some level of debt service cover ratio).	Mitigating the demand risk; increasing the revenue volume and stability.		X
	3.2 Guarantee in case of default, to cover the payment of outstanding debt (both principal and interest) in the case of private player's default.	Providing credit enhancement; increasing the overall funding available, and/or reducing the interest rate applied on the debt.	X	X
	3.3 Guarantee in case of refinancing, to repay lenders if the SPV fails to refinance the loan at maturity, especially in the event of increased interest rates or changed market liquidity.	Providing credit enhancement; increasing the overall funding available, and/or reducing the interest rate applied on the debt.		X
4. Provision of capital	4.1 Subordinated (junior) debt	Enhancing the credit quality of the senior debt, increasing the overall funding available, and/or reducing the interest rate applied on the senior debt.	X	
	4.2 Debt: 4.2.1 at pari passu condition 4.2.2 at lower interest rate (concessional money)	Providing debt capital at competitive market condition; in some circumstances, it can be provided also at lower rates, thus helping the project to meet the expectation of other debt capital investors, in terms of interest rate, DSCR, and maturity.	X	
	4.3 Equity: 4.3.1 at market conditions 4.3.2 at more advantageous conditions (concessional money)	Providing equity to fill the equity gap; reducing the financial leverage, and, therefore, the exposure to credit risk.	X	
	5. Favorable taxation schemes for SPV	Introducing lower corporate taxation to sustain the general viability of the project (i.e., increasing free cash flow from operation).		X

DSCR = debt service cover ratio, SPV = special purpose vehicle.

Source: Adapted from V. Vecchi, M. Hellowell, and F. Casalini. 2017. Issues and Trends in Project Finance for Public Infrastructure. In S. Caselli and S. Gatti, eds. *Structured Finance: Techniques, Products and Market.* Springer International Publishing (pp. 127–152).

Box 9 offers an overview of the total lending and guarantees provided by governments and government agencies, MDBs, DFIs, as well as other guarantee organizations to support infrastructure funding in both developed and developing markets, alongside some examples of projects and programs put in place by MDBs in emerging countries.

Box 9: An Overview of Multilateral Development Lending and Guarantees to Infrastructure

Project finance multilateral activity in developing countries, with 106 deals, reached a total exposure of $19.3 billion, of which $17.1 billion was for direct lending and $2.2 billion was for guarantees in 2020 (Table). As for the total exposure, there was a decrease of 19% compared to 2019, when the number of deals was 173 with $21.1 billion of direct loans and $9.2 billion of guarantees. Despite collapsed in emerging markets with the insurgence of the pandemic, but with a rebound in Q3 2021, guarantees have been recognized as effective instruments to mobilize private capital,[a] mitigating various types of risks that can undermine the bankability of infrastructure projects.

Table: Project Finance Multilateral Activity and Number of Deals, 2017–Q3 2021
($ million)

		Developing Market	Developed Market
Q3 2021	Direct Lending	5.943	3.945
	Guarantees	3.903	98
	Total Exposure	9.846	4.043
	No. of Deals	73	25
2020	Direct Lending	17.134	5.715
	Guarantees	2.247	5.256
	Total Exposure	19.381	10.971
	No. of Deals	106	35
2019	Direct Lending	21.187	2.392
	Guarantees	9.284	752
	Total Exposure	30.472	3.143
	No. of Deals	173	19
2018	Direct Lending	14.721	5.712
	Guarantees	6.558	4.086
	Total Exposure	21.279	9.798
	No. of Deals	158	34

Q3 = third quarter.
Source: Refinitiv Deal Intelligence.

An example of a project which benefited from guarantees provided by multilateral development bank (MDBs) was the Azura-Edo open-cycle gas turbine power project (459 megawatts), Nigeria's first privately developed, greenfield, limited recourse project-financed independent power producer. The project reached the financial close in 2015 and began generating electricity in 2017. The state-owned Nigeria Bulk Electricity Trader (NBET) is the off-taker of the plant under a 20-year power purchase agreement. The project raised $876 million in funding through equity investors (20%) and debt financers (80%), but called for a complex package of guarantees to be bankable, provided by the Multilateral Investment Guarantee Agency (MIGA) and the International Bank for Reconstruction and Development (IBRD). Specifically, MIGA arranged guarantees ($492 million)[b] against political risks (S&P B+ in 2015), covering equity investors and commercial lenders, while IBRD contributed with a payment guarantee to backstop NBET's payment security obligations ($120 million) and debt mobilization guarantee, which facilitated the sponsors to secure a tranche of commercial debt ($118 million).[c]

Another example of project was Türkiye's Elazig Hospital, a greenfield public–private partnership (PPP) project for improving access to health-care services in Eastern Anatolia, which reached the financial close in 2016. The

Box 9 *(continued)*

project was cited by the Global Infrastrucuture Hub as an example of the application of the G20 Principles for Quality Infrastructure Investment.[d] The Turkish Ministry of Health awarded a 28-year concession to the project company to design, build, finance, equip, and maintain the hospital, with a mechanism for payments comprised of availability and service payments.[e] The project company raised €360 million in funds, of which 80% (€288 million) financed by the issuance of a project bond that was placed with global investors, including FMO and Proparco.[f] Development financing support was mainly provided through a 20-year political risk guarantee in support of the investment-grade portion of the bond (€208 million) and guarantee to equity investment, both offered by MIGA. Furthermore, the project bond benefited from two unfunded subordinated liquidity facilities (€89 million) provided by the European Bank for Reconstruction and Development. This credit enhancement contributed to the Baa2 rating of the bond by Moody's, which was two notches higher than Türkiye's sovereign debt rating.

Examples of programs to attract institutional investors and support a pipeline of infrastructure projects implemented by MDBs include the Fondo Nacional de Infraestructura (FONADIN), a fund created by the Mexican government within Banobras, the largest MDB of Mexico; and the Credit Guarantee and Investment Facility (CGIF), established by the 10 members of the Association of Southeast Asian Nations (ASEAN) together with the People's Republic of China, Japan, the Republic of Korea (collectively known as ASEAN+3), and the Asian Development Bank.

FONADIN provides financial guarantees to both Mexican states and Mexican municipalities that are keen to implement infrastructure-based PPPs as well as directly to infrastructure projects. They are designed to enhance private participation in the financing of infrastructure, and they include the following:

- **Securities debt guarantees.** These guarantees can be used to support bonds issued to the market by project developers.

- **Bank guarantees.** These guarantees support the debt service the project must pay to a bank due to contracted loans.

- **Guarantees for service provision projects.** These guarantees are intended to cover the periodic payment obligations of the contracting units derived from the service provision contracts signed with the suppliers of the service.

- **Pari passu guarantees.** These are other similar schemes with the main difference that losses are assumed pro rata between Banobras and commercial banks.

FONADIN also supports medium-sized Mexican concessionaires in the energy and construction sector through equity investments, with the aim to help them compete with international or larger sponsors.

CGIF is part of the Asian Bond Markets Initiative and serves to provide credit guarantees for local-currency-denominated bonds issued by companies (including special purpose vehicles [SPVs] for the development of infrastructure) in ASEAN+3 countries. CGIF offers construction period guarantees to issuers of project bonds and secures the completion of construction works and commencement of operations of greenfield infrastructure projects. If the construction phase is not successfully completed, CGIF reimburses bondholders all amounts owed to them by SPVs. Due to CGIF´s due diligence process in the course of providing the guarantee, investors are assured that construction risks are well assessed and covered.

[a] OECD. 2020. Amounts mobilized from private sector by development finance interventions 2012–2019.
[b] World Bank Group. 2017. Nigeria: The Azura-Edo Independent Power Plant.
[c] World Bank Group. 2018. Nigeria Azura-Edo IPP.
[d] Global Infrastructure Hub. 2021. Elazig Hospital PPP.
[e] Industrial and Commercial Bank of China. 2021. Turkey Hospital PPP Project.
[f] World Bank Group. 2017. Turkey: Elazig Hospital.

While these instruments provides de-risking mechanisms and expand lending at project level, governments and MDBs can also implement blended finance mechanisms, to mobilize lending at system level. In particular, MDBs can play a role in expanding lending to infrastructure through project finance securitization (see Section 5.3) in two main ways:

- MDBs can leverage project finance CLO transactions to repackage the risk of their portfolio of project finance loans and increase lending capacity to infrastructure projects without requiring additional capital contributions from shareholder governments.

- MBDs can leverage project finance CLO structuring mechanisms by taking on subordinated first-loss tranches of the capital structure, as shown in Figure 18; this mechanism enhances the credit quality of the senior notes and attracts private institutional investors by providing them with comfort and confidence in the transaction.

Figure 18: An Example of Blending Mechanism to Support Project Finance Securitization

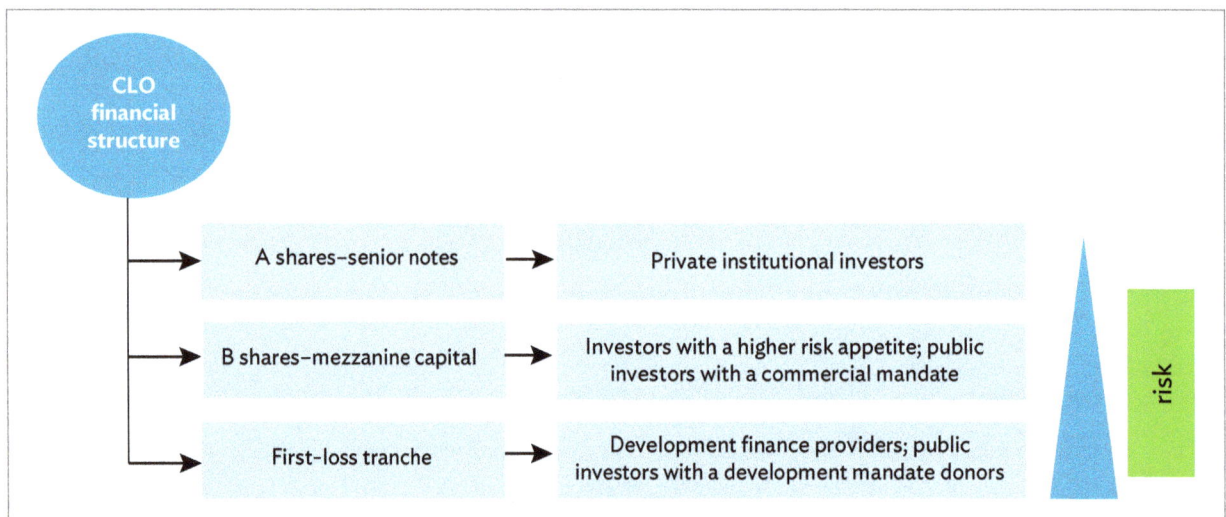

CLO = collateralized loan obligation.
Source: Adapted from V. Vecchi, F. Casalini, and N. Cusumano. 2021. Public-Private Collaborations for Long-Term Investments. Policies and investments approaches. Edward Elgar Publishing. In press.

Box 10 describes the case of the synthetic securitization of a pool of loans originated by the African Development Bank. This case is relevant for two reasons: first, it is a repackaging of loans originated by an MDB, to reduce capital requirements and increase lending capacity to infrastructure in Africa; second, the project finance CLO transaction is supported by mezzanine capital provided by public investors with a development mandate (e.g., Africa50 and the European Commission).

The abovementioned de-risking measures at project level are not alternatives to blended finance mechanisms, since they offer support to specific projects and, therefore, can be combined with blended mechanisms to sustain a stable capital attraction to infrastructure lending at system level. Pooling techniques, i.e., the bundling of a portfolio of different project finance loans, are beneficial not only in terms of default risk diversification, but also to match the large investment size needed by institutional investors. This could prove particularly helpful in smaller economies with limited deal flow, and in countries with nascent PPP programs.

Box 10: Capital Relief for Expanding Infrastructure Lending: The Synthetic Securitization of the African Development Bank and Cooperation among Public and Private Investors

Short description of the transaction

A promising application of securitization has been the Room-to-Run (R2R) program of the African Development Bank (AfDB), which is the first portfolio synthetic securitization between a multilateral development bank (MDB) and private investors, which was closed in September 2018.[a] The purpose of the R2R program was to enable the AfDB to expand the lending capacity, redeploying freed-up capital in renewable energy projects across the African continent without requiring supplementary capital from shareholders.

Overview of the portfolio

The transaction shifted the mezzanine credit risk on nonsovereign loans worth $1 billion to private investors. The reference portfolio pooled by AfDB consisted of 45 seasoned pan-African loans,[b] denominated in multiple currencies, to power, transportation, manufacturing, and financial sectors[c] with an average rating of B- and an average maturity of 6 years.[d]

Key transaction parties involved

Mizuho International structured the portfolio creating four different tranches: a senior tranche worth $727.5 million, a senior mezzanine tranche worth $100 million, a mezzanine tranche worth $152.5 million, and a junior tranche worth $20 million (Figure) (footnote d). Mariner, a global alternative asset manager, was the anchor investor in the transaction through its International Infrastructure Finance Company II fund (IIFC II). Africa50, the pan-African infrastructure investment platform, invested alongside Mariner in the mezzanine tranche. Moreover, the European Commission provided supplementary credit protection through the European Fund for Sustainable Development.

Figure: The Room-to-Run Synthetic Securitization Deal

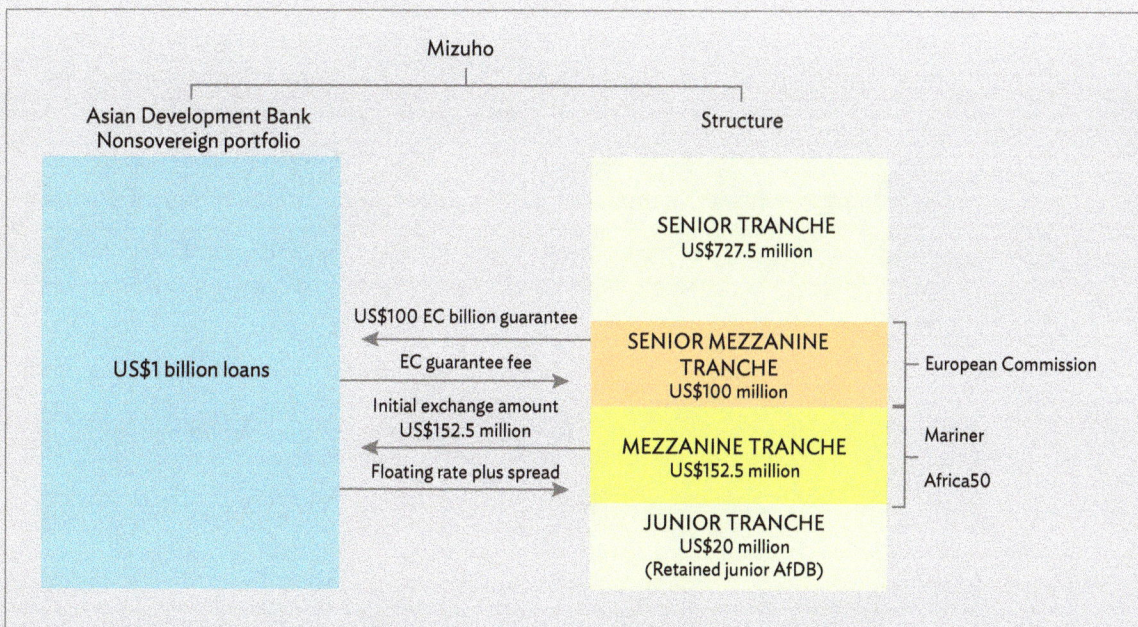

AfDB = African Development Bank, EC = European Commission, US = United States.
Source: The Rockefeller Foundation (2020).

Box 10 *(continued)*

Investor profiles

The IIFC II fund focuses on regulatory capital transactions, typically targeting infrastructure loans held by global financial institutions. With a size of $630 million, the fund's investments are structured as impact investments to incorporate principles related to socially responsible investment.

Africa50 is a listed infrastructure investment vehicle co-managed by AfDB and the Made in Africa Foundation to catalyze funding for local African infrastructure development. As an open-ended fund, Africa50 comprises a project development arm targeting $500 million, and a project finance arm, which aims to raise approximately $10 billion further down the line. The fund targets core greenfield and brownfield infrastructure within the power, roads, railway, telecommunications, and utilities sectors through equity and debt investments.

Key results and lessons learned

As a consequence of the synthetic securitization, AfDB maintained the 2% of losses in the reference portfolio, buying mezzanine risk protection for the 15.25% tranche from Mariner and Africa50, totaling $152.5 million that AfDB received as notional amount. With a credit enhancement in the form of a credit risk guarantee on the senior mezzanine tranche, the European Commission covered losses between 17.25% and 27.25% (foonote c). In exchange for mezzanine risk protection, AfDB pays investors a floating rate plus a spread and a guarantee fee to the European Commission. The transaction generated a reduction of risk-weighted assets of the portfolio for AfDB, which was equivalent to supplementary lending of $650 million, while maintaining its credit rating. The rating agency Standard & Poor's calculated the impact of the transaction through its Risk Adjusted Capital Framework for supranational.

Despite the difficulty to reach a critical mass of assets to justify a securitization in developing countries, given its underlying costs and the need of multiple loan originators to allow the scalability of the model (possibly seeing MDBs collaborating in joint securitization), the transaction has demonstrated multiple advantages:

- Securitizing a loan portfolio into separate tranches with varying degrees of underlying credit default risk, provides different risk and return attributes suitable for multiple investor profiles (for instance, mezzanine tranches for Africa50 whose investments strategy includes mezzanine debt).

- The transaction can generate increased lending capacity at MDBs without requiring capital contributions from shareholder governments (for example, $ 650 million of freed-capital for AfDB).

- Specifically synthetic securitization, wherein the loans remain on the balance sheets, ensures that MDBs measure and report on development of the financed projects, maintaining the relationship with the borrowers.

[a] OECD. 2021. Making blended finance work for sustainable development: The role of risk transfer mechanisms.
[b] The Rockefeller Foundation. 2020. A sustainable development certificates framework.
[c] OECD. 2020. Blended finance principle 4 guidance: Focus on effective partnering for blended finance.
[d] Gabor, D. 2019. *Securitization for Sustainability: Does it help achieve the Sustainable Development Goals?* Washington, DC: Heinrich Boll Stiftung.

7

CONCLUSION

This report explores possible forms of cooperation between banks and institutional investors aiming to increase lending to infrastructure finance, taking into consideration the mechanisms under which public institutions can improve the risk profile of infrastructure investments in order to enhance its attractiveness for private capital. The unprecedented social and economic consequences of the pandemic have reinforced the pressure on institutional investors to reduce the infrastructure financing gap. The main findings of the report are as follows:

- As long as recovery policy efforts include government stimulus packages for increased investment in infrastructure, there is a significant opportunity to upgrade existing infrastructure stock and to build new infrastructure to address short- and long-term challenges. Indeed, there is consensus between public and private stakeholders regarding the increasingly pivotal role of infrastructure in ambitious and urgent climate and development goals, and in the sustainable recovery from the pandemic, such as through digital connectivity, robust utility infrastructure, and health-care provision.

- However, the pandemic can exacerbate the challenges of underinvesting in infrastructure projects both in developed and developing countries. Governments have been facing unprecedented levels of debt due to extraordinary fiscal policies, while banks have been concerned about a rebound in corporate defaults that could cause a deterioration in the quality of their loan portfolios, including nonperforming loans and credit losses, accompanied by a potential reduction of their capital adequacy coefficients.

- Therefore, traditional sources of funding from governments and banks would not be sufficient to address the demand for infrastructure financing, reinforcing the pressure on institutional investors to narrow the gap. In fact, it is commonly agreed that investors with long-term liabilities and low risk appetite seem suited to invest in infrastructure assets with a low risk profile. In particular, investors are interested in purchasing infrastructure assets to diversify their portfolios because of the low correlation of infrastructure with traditional asset classes. Moreover, the investment characteristics of infrastructure are associated with predictable (i.e., long-term contracts) and stable (i.e., low volatility or inelastic demand) cash flows over the long term, and are inflation-hedged. Infrastructure investments can thus represent an effective asset–liability management strategy.

- While market analyses suggest that unlisted equity funds are the prevailing vehicle of institutional infrastructure financing, private debt has become a growing component of their infrastructure asset management. In this context, institutional investors' debt financing has increased mainly through project bond issuance, but also through different co-investment models with banks. Under this approach, banks originate a transaction to "re-sell" or "distribute" the infrastructure debt to investors instead of keeping the assets on their balance sheet until maturity. Pooling techniques (e.g., CLOs) in capital markets can support investors and banks to close the infrastructure financing gap. Specifically, from an institutional investor's perspective, securitized debt portfolios can be tailored to their risk-and-return profiles, offering risk diversification advantages. From a bank's perspective, by moving project finance loans from the bank balance sheets and transferring the credit risk of the underlying loan portfolio to bond investors via securitization, project finance CLOs accelerate loan issuance, and free up bank lending capacity (i.e., asset recycling) to infrastructure.

- However, despite the growing interest of institutional investors to the asset class, infrastructure investments still represent a small fraction of their managed assets. Several challenges are faced by emerging markets and developing economies, ranging from sovereign risk to regulatory uncertainty, that can impede the achievement of the threshold investment grade rating required by long-term institutional investors. Nonetheless, governments, DFIs, and MDBs can play a role as part of the enabling ecosystem across the infrastructure project life cycle, as well as in facilitating private sector investments into infrastructure. For instance, MDBs can bolster the lending capacity to infrastructure through project finance securitization and suitable guarantees by assisting banks in securitizing their loan portfolios for projects in emerging markets and developing economies or by pooling their own portoflios (e.g., African Development Bank).

REFERENCES

Abiad, A. et al. 2020. The Impact of COVID-19 on Developing Asia: The Pandemic Extends into 2021. *ADB Briefs*. Manila: Asian Development Bank.

Airport Council International. 2021. The impact of Covid-19 on the airport business and the path to recover.

Allen & Overy. 2021. Institutional Investor Forum 2021. How I Made It.

Asian Development Bank (ADB). 2017. *Meeting Asia's Infrastructure Needs*. Manila.

———. 2021. *Asian Development Outlook (ADO) 2021: Financing a Green and Inclusive Recovery*. Manila.

———. 2022. *Asian Development Outlook (ADO) 2022 Supplement: Recovery Faces Diverse Challenges*. Manila

Asian Infrastructure Investment Bank. 2020. Asian Infrastructure Finance 2020: Investing Better, Investing More.

Association for Financial Markets in Europe. 2020. Capital Markets Union: Key Performance Indicators - Third edition.

Axelson, U., T. Jenkinson, P. Strömberg, and M. Weisbach. 2013. Borrow Cheap, Buy High? The Determinants of Leverage and Pricing in Buyouts. *The Journal of Finance*. 68(6). pp. 2223–67.

Bachher, J., and A. Monk. 2013. Platforms and Vehicles for Institutional Co-Investing. *Rotman International Journal of Pension Management, 6(1)*.

Berger, R. 2017. Implication of Ongoing "Basel IV" Debates: Significant New Constraints to Come for Banks, with Expected Ramifications for European Economy Financing.

Blanc-Brude, F., A. Chreng, M. Hasan, Q. Wang, and T. Whittaker. 2017. Private Infrastructure Debt Broad Market Indices: Benchmarking Europe's Private Infrastructure Debt Market 2000–2016. Singapore: EDHEC Infrastructure Institute.

Buscaino, V., S. Caselli, F. Corielli, and S. Gatti. 2012. Project finance collateralised debt obligations: An empirical analysis of spread determinants. *European Financial Management*. 18(5). pp. 950–969.

Cambridge Associates. 2018. Infrastructure debt: Understanding the opportunity.

Clark, G. et al. 2012. The New Era of Infrastructure Investing. *Pensions: An International Journal*. 17(2). pp. 103–11.

Creswell, J. W., and C. N. Poth. 2016. *Qualitative Inquiry and Research Design*. Fourth Edition. Los Angeles; London; New Delhi; Singapore; Washington, DC: SAGE.

Della Croce, R., and S. Gatti. 2014. *Financing Infrastructure: International Trends*. Paris: Organisation for Economic Co-operation and Development (OECD).

Della Croce, R., and R. Sharma. 2014. Pooling of Institutional Investors Capital: Selected case studies in unlisted equity infrastructure. OECD.

The Economist Intelligence Unit. 2019. The critical role of infrastructure for the Sustainable Development Goals.

European PPP Expertise Centre. 2021. Financing PPPs with project bonds. Luxembourg: EPEC.

Fang, L., V. Ivashina, and J. Lerner. 2015. The Disintermediation of Financial Markets: Direct Investing in Private Equity. *Journal of Financial Economics*. 116(1). pp. 160–78.

Financial Stability Board. 2018. Evaluation of the effects of financial regulatory reforms on infrastructure finance.

Fitch Ratings. 2020. Credit Costs to Remain Elevated for APAC Banks in 2021.

Fitch Ratings. 2020. Fitch Ratings 2021 Outlook: Asia-Pacific Emerging Market Banks.

G20. 2015. Multilateral Development Banks Action Plan to Optimize Balance Sheets.

G20. 2019. G20 Principles for Quality Infrastructure Investment.

G20 Sustainable Finance Working Group. 2018. Towards a Sustainable Infrastructure Securitisation Market: The Role of Collateralised Loan Obligations (CLO).

Gabor, D. 2019. *Securitization for Sustainability: Does It Help Achieve the Sustainable Development Goals?* Washington, DC: Heinrich Boll Stiftung.

Gatti, S. 2018. *Project Finance in Theory and Practice: Designing, Structuring, and Financing Private and Public Projects*. Third Edition. London: Elsevier, Academic Press.

Gatti, S. 2020. *Basel IV Impact on Specialized Lending and Project Finance*. Milan: SDA Bocconi School of Management. Bocconi University.

Global Infrastructure Hub. 2020. Fiscal multiplier effect of infrastructure investment.

Global Infrastructure Hub. 2021. Elazig Hospital PPP.

Grushkin, J., and D. Bartfeld. 2013. Securitizing Project Finance Loans: Are PF CLOs Poised for a Comeback? *The Journal of Structured Finance*. 19(3). pp. 76–81

Hallak, I., and M. Wambeke. 2014. The New Landscape of the Infrastructure Debt Market: Opportunities for Banks and Institutional Investors. Vlerick Business School. Gent.

Industrial and Commercial Bank of China. 2021. Turkey Hospital PPP Project.

Infrastructure Investor. 2021. Debt report.

International Energy Agency. 2021. Global energy review 2021.

International Labour Organization. 2021. World Employment and Social Outlook. Trends 2021.

International Monetary Fund (IMF). 2021. Fiscal Monitor.

———. 2021. Global Financial Stability Report.

———. 2021. Policy Advice to Asia in the COVID-19 Era.

———. 2021. World Economic Outlook. Managing Divergent Recoveries.

International Telecommunication Union. 2020. Economic impact of Covid-19 on digital infrastructure.

Kaplan, S., and A. Schoar. 2005. Private Equity Performance: Returns, Persistence, and Capital Flows. *The Journal of Finance.* 60(4), pp. 1791–1823.

Ma, T. 2016. Basel III and the Future of Project Finance Funding. *Michigan Business & Entrepreneurial Law Review.* 6(1), pp. 109–126.

McKinsey & Company. 2019. Signs of Stress. Is Asia Heading Towards a Debt Crisis?

———. 2020. How healthy is the Asian financial system?

———. 2020. Reimagining emerging ASEAN in the wake of COVID-19.

Mirabile, M., V. Marchal, and R. Baron. 2017. Technical note on estimates of infrastructure investment needs. OECD.

Monk, A., and R. Sharma. 2015. Re-Intermediating Investment Management: A Relational Contracting Approach. *Stanford Global Projects Center Working Paper.*

Moody's. 2020. Infrastructure Default and Recovery Rates 1983–2019.

Natixis Investment Managers. 2021. 2021 Global Institutional Investors Outlook. Into the great wide open.

Organisation for Economic Co-operation and Development (OECD). 2014. Pooling of Institutional Investors Capital - Selected Case Studies in Unlisted Equity Infrastructure.

———. 2015. Infrastructure Financing Instruments and Incentives.

———. 2015. Risk and Return characteristics of infrastructure investment in low income countries.

———. 2020. Amounts mobilized from the private sector for development.

———. 2020. Blended finance principle 4 guidance: Focus on effective partnering for blended finance.

———. 2021. Annual Survey of Large Pension Funds and Public Pension Reserve Funds.

———. 2021. COVID-19 and a new resilient infrastructure landscape.

———. 2021. G20/OECD Report on the collaboration with institutional investors and asset managers on infrastructure.

———. 2021. Insurance Statistics 2020.

———. 2021. Making blended finance work for sustainable development: The role of risk transfer mechanisms.

———. 2021. OECD Economic Outlook.

———. 2021. Pension Funds in Figures.

Preqin. 2021. Global Infrastructure Report.

———. 2021. Investor Outlook Alternative Assets H1 2021.

———. 2021. Preqin Quarterly Update: Infrastructure Q1 2021.

Probitas Partners. 2020. Infrastructure Institutional Investor Trends: 2019 Survey Results.

The Rockefeller Foundation. 2020. A sustainable development certificates framework.

Sawada, Y., and R. Sumulong.2021. Macroeconomic Impact of Covid-19 in Developing Asia. *ADBI Working Papers*. No. 1251. Tokyo: Asian Development Bank Institute.

Seawright, J., and J. Gerring. 2008. Case Selection Techniques in Case Study Research: A Menu of Qualitative and Quantitative Options. *Political Research Quarterly*. 61 (2). pp. 294–308.

Swiss Re Group. 2020. Post-COVID recovery: Infrastructure in Emerging Asia holds the key.

Swiss Re Group. 2021. Closing the Infrastructure Gap. Mobilising Institutional Investment into Sustainable, Quality Infrastructure in Emerging Markets and Developing Economies (EMDEs).

UBS Asset Management. 2020. Infrastructure outlook: Light at the end of the tunnel?

United Nations Conference on Trade and Development (UNCTAD). Impact of the COVID-19 pandemic on trade and development (March 2021).

Vecchi, V., F. Casalini, and N. Cusumano. 2021. Public-Private Collaborations for Long-Term Investments. Policies and investments approaches. Edward Elgar Publishing. In press.

Vecchi, V., M. Hellowell, and F. Casalini. 2017. Issues and Trends in Project Finance for Public Infrastructure. In S. Caselli and S. Gatti (Eds.), *Structured Finance: Techniques, Products and Market* (pp. 127–152).

Vecchi, V., M. Hellowell, R. Della Croce, and S. Gatti. 2017. Government Policies to Enhance Access to Credit for Infrastructure-based PPPs: An Approach to Classification and Appraisal. *Public Money & Management.* 37 (2). pp. 133-140.

Verhoest, K., O. Petersen, W. Scherrer, and R. M. Soecipto. 2015. How Do Governments Support the Development of Public Private Partnerships? Measuring and Comparing PPP Governmental Support in 20 European Countries. *Transport Reviews.* 35 (2). pp. 118-139.

Walter, I. 2016. *The Infrastructure Finance Challenge: A Report by the Working Group on Infrastructure Finance.* Stern School of Business, New York University.

White & Case. LLP. 2021. Eye on the future: The outlook for Asian infrastructure.

World Bank. 2017. Turkey: Elazig Hospital.

————. 2018. Nigeria: The Azura-Edo Independent Power Plant.

————. 2020. Infrastructure financing in times of Covid-19: A driver for recovery.

————. 2020. Private Participation in Infrastructure (PPI): 2020 Annual Report.

————. 2022. Worldwide Governance Indicators.

World Economic Forum. 2013. Strategic Infrastructure. Steps to Prepare and Accelerate Public-Private Partnerships.

World Health Organization. 2021. Coronavirus dashboard (accessed 30 September 2022).

Wouter, T., and L. De Moor. 2019. Loan Tenor in Project Finance. *International Journal of Managing Projects in Business.* 12 (3). pp. 825-842.

Yescombe, E. R. 2013. *Principles of Project Finance.* Second Edition. London: Elsevier, Academic Press.

www.ingramcontent.com/pod-product-compliance
Lightning Source LLC
Chambersburg PA
CBHW050050220326
41599CB00045B/7354